Chrismons™

Crosses & Crowns

INSTRUCTIONS FOR MAKING HOME SIZE CHRISMONS

Adapted from the designs by Frances Kipps Spencer

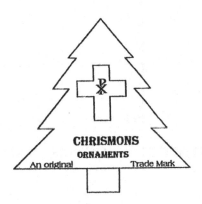

Chrismons speak of our Lord Jesus Christ. Ascension Lutheran Church welcomes you to the growing family of those who make and use these Christian ornaments. May you find the peace of God and joy in His Word as you work with these reminders of His love for all mankind.

The patterns and descriptions given are adapted from the original patterns of the church size Chrismons that hang on the tree in our church. We hope that you will enjoy making Chrismons, that you will find happiness in using them and in giving them to others. Our only limitation is that they not be made for sale.

If you wish to use Chrismons in a church or a non-profit institution we are glad, on request to send that organization full permission to use any of our materials (copyright or otherwise) to explain the meaning of the ornaments. Simply send your request with the name and address of the church or institution to us. The copyright release will be forwarded at once.

May God bless you in your desire to keep our Lord at the center of your Christmas celebration.

**From the Chrismons Ministry Team
at Ascension Lutheran Church
Danville, Virginia, U.S.A.**

CREDITS

PHOTOGRAPHS:

Heather F. Vipperman, Kate Albright

PUBLICATION:

Pastor Meredith Williams

Kate Albright

Heidi Kefauver

Heather F. Vipperman

> **Chrismons are:**
>
> Christmas tree ornaments that declare the name, the life, and the saving acts of Jesus the Christ.
>
> They are made in the colors of
>
> White, to suggest the innocence, purity and perfection of our Savior
>
> And
>
> Gold, to as a symbol of the glory and majesty of God and the Son of God.

Chrismons: Crosses and Crowns

First Edition

First Printing

Copyright© 2014 by the Evangelical Lutheran Church of the Ascension,

Danville, Virginia. All rights reserved.

Published by the Ascension Lutheran Church

314 West Main Street, Danville, Virginia 24541, U.S.A.

Printed in the United States of America

ISBN 978-0-9715472-7-8

www.chrismon.org   chrismon@gamewood.net   434-792-5795

Table of Contents

* First Publication of this pattern

This book is dedicated to women and men who have embraced the Chrismons Ministry and shared the message through the designs of Mrs. Francis Kipps Spencer.

Chrismon Secretaries

Leona M. Buettner 1967—2000

Steven Cooper 2000—2012

Heather F. Vipperman 2012—2015

Tools

Kneedle Nose Pliers	Wire Cutters
Large embroidery needle	Pencil
Empty fruit cup containers	Toothpick
Felt or Jeweler's cloth for placemat	

Basics Steps used

Crossover - The **Crossover** step may be abbreviated **C/O or CC** (Chris Cross) in patterns.

1. To begin, feed two beads the center of a wire.
2. Add a third bead to one wire. Take the opposite wire and feed back through the bead so the wires "crossover" each other inside the bead.
3. Pull tight.

Left wire through bead exit right

Right wire through same bead exit left

Mouse Ears - Similar to the Crossover step, "Mouse Ears" are used to make a wider end on an element of the ornament. Examples include the Flared Latin Cross.

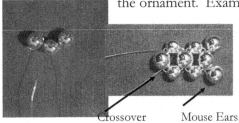

Crossover   Mouse Ears

1. Begin with one bead centered on the wire.
2. Add a second bead and return weave into the first bead.
3. Add a third bead on the remaining wire and return weave into the first bead creating "Mouse Ears".

Chrismons™ Ornaments

Ascension Lutheran Church 314 West Main Street
Danville, Virginia 24540 Phone: 434-792-5795
Web: chrismon.org, Facebook, Pinterest, Etsy
E-mail: chrismonsministry@gmail.com
Copyright 2016 Lutheran Church of the Ascension, Danville, VA

Alpha Lambda Cross

Difficulty: Intermediate

Finished size: 3.25 inches

Beads:

4 4mm pearl

4 2mm gold

165 3mm gold

Wires:

2 14-inch 28 gauge gold

4 7-inch 28 gauge gold

1 11-inch 28 gauge gold

Chrismons
(CHRISt + MONogramS)

Alpha Lambda Cross
With four Crosslets

In the beginning was the Word, and the Word was with God and the Word was God. *John 1:1*

Alpha is the first letter of the Greek alphabet and reminds us of the beginning. Lambda is the first letter of the Greek *Logos* - Word.

The four crosslets represent the Great Commission. The crossbar of the A reminds us of outstretched arms.

Go therefore and make disciples of all the nations, baptizing them in the name of the Father and the Son and the Holy Spirit, teaching them to observe all that I have commanded you. And behold, I am with you always, to the end of the age.
Matthew 28:19-20

Ascension Lutheran Church
Danville, Virginia

In the beginning was the Word, and the Word was with God, and the Word was God.

John 1:1

Alpha is the first letter of the Greek alphabet and has been used in other symbols to direct our thoughts to the beginning. We have the self-description of God in *Revelations 1:8 "I am the Alpha and the Omega,"* says the Lord God, "who is and who was and who is to come, the Almighty."

Within the A is also lambda, the beginning letter for the Greek word logos, which means word. In Paul's epistles, he refers to the gospel message as logos. Christ has also been identified as the Word.

And the Word became flesh and dwelt among us, and we have seen his glory, glory as of the only Son from the Father, full of grace and truth. John 1:14.

The crossbar of the letter A is extended to resemble the cross arm of the cross, which holds us in its embrace, having been transformed by Jesus' sacrifice from an instrument of torture into a symbol of hope. The number 4 has been used in Christian art to indicate the four corners of the earth, in other words, the whole world. The crosslets therefore refer to the Great Commission.

Matthew 28:19-20. Go therefore and make disciples of all nations, baptizing them in the name of the Father and of the Son and of the Holy Spirit, teaching them to observe all that I have commanded you. And behold, I am with you always, to the end of the age."

Another level of meaning is to see the A and the L, the Latin equivalent of lambda, as representing Ascension Lutheran Church, as we are part of the body of Christ. The words of John and of Matthew are directed to us personally, not as some sort of historical legacy of our faith. As we take on the Great Commission by having the Chrismons ministry, we are engaged in extending the Gospel message to the ends of the earth, as answered by other Chrismons from all the inhabited continents. As Frances Spencer noted, our tree is not complete until we have explained its meaning to others. Therefore, unless we embrace others by our Christian witness, we have not finished the task we have chosen for ourselves.

A third level of meaning may be found in the shape, which is five-pointed and has a roughly human form. This also reminds us of John 1:14 that Jesus became flesh and dwelt among us. This can also refer to the Lutheran doctrine of the goodness of God's creation and its ongoing nature. As this shape is incorporated into the overall design, it is reflective of Jesus' totally human and totally divine nature, inseparable and coexistent. It also speaks to Jesus' sacrifice, as the number 5 can symbolize the five wounds.

Alpha Leg (make 2)

1. Center three 3mm gold beads on 1 14-inch wire.
2. Crossover with one 3mm gold bead.
3. Add one 3mm gold bead to each wire.
4. Crossover with one 4mm pearl bead.
5. Add one 3mm gold bead to each wire.
6. Crossover with one 3mm gold bead. Repeat until you have 12 crossovers above the pearl bead.
7. Set aside and make second leg.

Attach Alpha legs

1. Thread 1 wire from each Alpha leg straight up into one 3mm gold bead.
2. Add one 3 mm gold bead to second wire of each leg.
3. Crossover with two 3mm gold beads on each side of the center bead.
4. Repeat one time.
5. Back weave outside wires until secure.
6. With remaining two center wires, crossover with 1 3mm gold bead.
7. Twist wires to secure.

Add Alpha crossbar

1. Center three 3mm gold beads on 11-inch gold wire. Crossover with one 3mm gold bead.
2. Add one 3mm gold bead to each wire. Crossover with one 4mm pearl bead.
3. Add one 3mm gold bead to each wire. Crossover with one 3mm gold bead.
4. Add one 3mm gold bead to each wire. Crossover with one 3mm gold bead.
5. Add one 3mm gold bead to upper wire, add one 2mm bead to lower wire.
6. Weave two wires through the 5th and 6th center beads counting up from the pearl bead.
7. Add one 2mm gold bead to upper wire, add one 3mm bead to lower wire, crossover with onc 3mm gold bead.
8. Add one 3mm gold bead to each wire. Crossover with one 3mm gold bead.
9. Add one 3mm gold bead to each wire. Crossover with one 3mm gold bead.
10. Add one 3mm gold bead to each wire. Crossover with one 3mm gold bead.
11. Add one 2mm gold bead to upper wire, add one 3mm bead to lower wire.
12. Weave two wires through the 5th and 6th center beads counting up from the pearl bead.
13. Add one 3mm gold bead to upper wire, add one 2mm bead to lower wire, crossover with one 3mm gold bead.
14. Add one 3mm gold bead to each wire. Crossover with one 3mm gold bead.
15. Add one 3mm gold bead to each wire. Crossover with one 4mm pearl bead.
16. Add one 3mm gold bead to each wire. Crossover with one 3mm gold bead.
17. Add one 3mm gold bead to each wire. Crossover with one 3mm gold bead.
18. Backweave to secure wires.

Add Four Crosslets

1. Center three 3mm gold beads on a 7-inch gold wire. Crossover with one 3mm gold bead.
2. Weave wires around a pearl bead as pictured at right.
3. Crossover with one 3mm gold bead.
4. Add one 3mm gold bead to each wire. Crossover with one 3mm gold bead.
5. Back weave to secure wires.
6. Repeat with each 7-inch wire and pearl.

Ascension Lutheran Church 314 West Main Street
Danville, Virginia 24540 Phone: 434-792-5795
Web: chrismon.org, Facebook, Pinterest, Etsy
E-mail: chrismonsministry@gmail.com
Copyright 2016 Lutheran Church of the Ascension, Danville, VA

Difficulty: Advanced

Finished size: 5.5 inches

Beads:

31	3mm pearl
2	4mm pearl
1	5mm pearl
34	6mm pearl
6	8mm pearl
1	10mm pearl
6	2mm gold
41	3mm gold
104	3x6mm gold

Wire

1 13-inch 26 gauge gold
1 23-inch 26 gauge gold
1 22-inch 28 gauge gold
4 10-inch 28 gauge gold

Chrismons
(CHRISt + MONogramS)
A Mother's Love

Cross, Heart and Love

The original of this design was created by Mrs. Francis Spencer from the beads of a carved ivory necklace that her mother wore when Mrs. Spencer was a child.

Mary treasured up all these things and pondered them in her heart. *Luke 2:19*

Love the Lord your God with all your heart and with all your soul and with all your strength and with all your mind; and Love your neighbor as yourself. *Luke 10:27*

Ascension Lutheran Church
Danville, VA

Upright of Cross *(starting at the bottom)*

1. Center one **8mm** pearl bead on the 22-inch 28-gauge gold wire.
2. Add one **3x6** gold bead to each wire and crossover with one **6mm** pearl bead.
3. *Repeat 3 times. At this point you have 1 8mm pearl and 4 6mm pearl beads.*
4. Add one **3x6** gold bead to each wire and crossover with one **5mm** pearl bead.
5. Add one **3x6** gold bead to each wire and crossover with one **3mm** gold bead.
6. Add one **3x6** gold bead to each wire and crossover with one **6mm** pearl bead.
7. *Repeat 3 times. At this point you have 1 8mm pearl. 4 6mm pearl, 1 5mm, 1 3mm gold and 4 6mm pearl .*
8. Add one **3x6** gold bead to each wire and crossover with one **10mm** pearl bead.
9. Add two **3mm** gold beads to each wire and crossover with one **4mm** pearl bead.
10. Add one **3x6** gold bead to each wire and crossover with one **6mm** pearl bead.
11. *Repeat 3 times. At this point you have 1 8mm pearl. 4 6mm pearl, 1 5mm, 1 3mm gold, 4 6mm pearl, 1 10mm*

pearl 1 4mm pearl and 4 6mm pearl.
12. Add one **3x6** gold bead to each wire and crossover with one **8mm** pearl bead.
13. Twist wires together for the hanger.

Crossbar of Cross

1. Center one **8mm** pearl bead on the 13-inch 26-gauge gold wire
2. Add one **3x6** gold bead to each wire and crossover with one **6mm** pearl bead.
3. *Repeat 3 times. At this point you have 1 8mm pearl and 4 6mm pearl beads.*
4. Add one **3x6** gold bead to the top wire and one **3mm** gold

bead to the bottom wire.

5. Weave the top wire up through the upright at upper **3mm** bead at the side of the **10mm** pearl bead, through the **4mm** pearl and down through the upper **3mm** gold bead on the other side of the **10mm** pearl bead.

6. Weave the bottom wire down through the upright at the **3x6** bead below the **10mm** pearl bead, through the 6mm pearl below the **10mm** pearl bead and up through the **3x6** bead on the other side of the **10mm** pearl bead.

7. Add one **3x6** gold bead to the top wire and one **3mm** gold bead to the bottom wire

8. crossover with one **6mm** pearl bead.

9. Add one **3x6** gold bead to each wire and crossover with one **6mm** pearl bead.

10. Repeat 2 times.

11. Add one **3x6** gold bead to each wire and crossover with one **8mm** pearl bead.   *At this point you have 1 8mm pearl and 4 6mm pearl beads on each side of the crossbar.*

12. Return weave to secure the wires.

Heart

1. Center one **6mm** pearl bead on the 23-inch 26-gauge wire.

2. Add one **3x6** gold bead to each wire and crossover with one **6mm** pearl bead.

3. Repeat 2 times.

4. Add one **3x6** gold bead to each wire, crossover in the **5mm** pearl bead on the upright. *At this point you have 4 6mm pearl beads on one side of the upright.*

5. Add one **3x6** gold bead to each wire and crossover with one **6mm** pearl bead.

6. Repeat 6 times.

7. Add one **3x6** gold bead to each wire and crossover with one **8mm** pearl bead.

8. Add one **2mm** gold bead and one **3x6** gold bead to each wire and crossover in the **10mm** pearl bead on the upright.   *At this point you have 4 6mm pearl beads on one side of the upright and 7 6mm pearls and 1 8mm pearl on the other side of the upright.*

9. Add one **3x6** gold bead and one **2mm** gold bead to each wire and crossover in one **8mm** pearl bead.

10. Add one **3x6** gold bead to each wire and crossover with one **6mm** pearl bead.

11. Repeat 2 times. *Both sides of the Heart should look the same.*

12. Return weave to secure the wires.

L

1. Center a 10-inch 28-gauge wire in the first **3x6** gold bead on the bottom left arm of the crossbar.

2. Add one **3mm** gold bead to each wire and

crossover with one **4mm** pearl bead.

3. Add one **3mm** gold bead to each wire and crossover with one **3mm** pearl bead.

4. Repeat 2 times.

5. Add two **3mm** gold beads to the outside wire and crossover with one **3mm** pearl bead.

6. Add one **3mm** gold bead to each wire and crossover with one **3mm** pearl bead.

7. Repeat 1 time and return weave to secure wires.

O

1. Thread a 10-inch wire through the upper third from the left **3x6** gold bead. Thread both wires down through the closest 6mm pearl. Thread the left wire through the lower third from the left **3x6** gold bead. Both wires should be below the third from the left **6mm** pearl bead.

2. Check that the wires are even. Crossover with one **3mm** gold bead.

3. Add one **3mm** pearl and 1 **3mm** gold bead to one wire, crossover with one **3mm** pearl bead.

4. Add one **3x6** gold bead to the outer wire and one **3mm** gold bead to the inner wire, crossover with one **3mm** pearl bead.

5. Add one **3x6** gold bead to each wire, crossover with one **3mm** pearl bead.

6. Add one **3x6** gold bead to the outer wire and one **3mm** gold bead to the inner wire, cross-

over with one **3mm** pearl bead.

7. Repeat 2 times.

8. Add one **3x6** gold bead to each wire, crossover with one **3mm** pearl bead.

9. Add one **3x6** gold bead to the outer wire and one **3mm** gold bead to the inner wire, crossover in the **3mm** pearl at the side of the top of the O.

10. Return weave to secure wires.

V

1. Center a 10-inch wire in the **3mm** gold bead on the lower portion of the crossbar, beside the **10mm** pearl.

2. Crossover in one **3mm** pearl bead.

3. Add 1 **3mm** gold bead to each wire and crossover with one **3mm** pearl bead.

4. Repeat 2 times.

5. Add two **3x6** gold beads to the outside wire, fold and shape **3x6** beads into V.

6. Crossover with one **3mm** pearl bead.

7. Add 1 **3mm** gold bead to each wire and crossover with one **3mm** pearl bead.

8. Repeat 2 times.

9. Crossover in third from the right side **3x6** gold bead on bottom of crossbar.

10. Return weave to secure wires.

E

1. Center a 10-inch wire in the last **3x6** gold bead on the bottom of the crossbar.
2. Add one **3mm** pearl and one **3x6** gold bead to the right wire, crossover with one **3mm** pearl bead.

3. Add one **2mm** gold bead to the left wire and crossover with one **3mm** pearl.
4. Add one **3x6** gold bead to each wire and crossover with one **3mm** pearl.
5. Add 1 **2mm** gold bead and 2 **3mm** pearl beads to the right wire. Thread wire down into the **2mm** gold bead again.
6. Add one **3x6** gold bead to each wire and crossover with one **3mm** pearl.
7. Add one **3mm** gold bead to the left wire and crossover with one **3mm** pearl bead.
8. Add one **3x6** gold bead to each wire and crossover with one **3mm** pearl.
9. Return weave to secure wires.

Photograph of the original A Mother's Love ornament made by Francis Kipps Spencer from carved ivory beads belonging to her mother.

Chrismons™ Ornaments

Ascension Lutheran Church 314 West Main Street
Danville, Virginia 24540 Phone: 434-792-5795
Web: chrismon.org Facebook, Pinterest, Etsy
E-mail: chrismonsministry@gmail.com
Copyright 2016 Lutheran Church of the Ascension, Danville, VA

Difficulty: Beginner

Finished size: 3.25 inches

Beads:

12 2mm pearl

6 3mm pearl

36 4mm pearl

8 5mm pearl

20 6mm pearl

2 8mm pearl

1 10mm pearl

Wire

2 18-inch 28 gauge silver

1 12-inch 28 gauge silver

Chrismons
(CHRISt + MONogramS)

The Anchor Cross
or
Cross of Hope

This Child,
the hope of the world.
A cross rises out of the
crescent moon,
a symbol for Mary, our
Lord's mother.

Ascension Lutheran Church
Danville, VA

Upright
1. Center 12 **2mm** beads on one 18-inch wire.
2. Cross-connect (CC) a **6mm** pearl.
3. Add a **4mm** bead on each wire and CC with a **6mm** bead.
4. Repeat 8 times. Do not cut wires. *You will have 10 **6mm** center beads.*

Arm
1. Center a 6mm bead on the 12-inch wire.
2. Add a **4mm** bead to each side and CC with a **6mm** bead.
3. Repeat one time. *You will have 3 **6mm** center beads.*
4. Attach the arm to the upright at the fourth **6mm** bead from the top.
5. On the other side CC with a **6mm** bead.
6. Add a **4mm** bead to each side and CC with a **6mm** bead.
7. Repeat one time. Secure and trim wires.

Crescent
1. Center a 3mm bead on an 18-inch wire.
2. Add a **3mm** bead to the upper wire and a **4mm** bead to the lower wire, CC with a **4mm**.
3. Add a **3mm** bead to the upper wire and a **4mm** bead to the lower wire, CC with a **5mm**.
4. Add a **4mm** bead to the upper wire and a **5mm** bead to the lower wire, CC with an **6mm**.
5. Add a **4mm** bead to the upper wire and a **5mm** bead to the lower wire, CC with an **8mm**.
6. Add a **5mm** bead to the upper

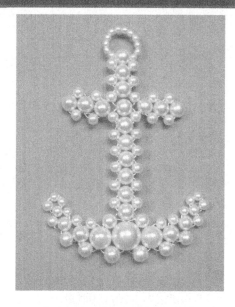

wire and a **6mm** bead to the lower wire, CC with a **10mm**.
7. Add a **5mm** bead to the upper wire and a **6mm** bead to the lower wire, CC with an **8mm**.
8. Add a **4mm** bead to the upper wire and a **5mm** bead to the lower wire, CC with an **6mm**
9. Add a **4mm** bead to the upper wire and a **5mm** bead to the lower wire, CC with a **5mm**.
10. Add a **3mm** bead to the upper wire and a **4mm** bead to the lower wire, CC with a **4mm**.
11. Add a **3mm** bead to the upper wire and a **4mm** bead on the lower wire, CC with a **3mm**.
12. Secure and trim wires.

Add Cross to Crescent.
1. Attach the cross to the inside of the crescent at the **10mm** pearl.
2. Thread the wires outward through the **5mm** beads, downward
3. through the **8mm** beads, outward through the **6mm** beads and
4. upward through the **6mm** pearls, trim wires.

Chrismons™ Ornaments

Ascension Lutheran Church 314 West Main Street
Danville, Virginia 24540 Phone: 434-792-5795
Web: chrismon.org Facebook, Pinterest, Etsy
E-mail: chrismonsministry@gmail.com
Copyright 2014 Lutheran Church of the Ascension, Danville, VA

Greek Cross

Difficulty: Beginner

Finished size: 4.25 inches

Beads:

45 6mm Pearl

12 8mm Pearl

Wires:

2 18 inch 28 gauge silver

Chrismons
(CHRISt + MONogramS)

Budded Greek Cross
or
Greek Cross Voided

The Greek cross has four equal arms representing the four corners of the earth, the four directions on the compass, or the four winds. Jesus brought salvation to people from ever direction and nation. *Mark 13:26 - 27*

The triple bud on the end of each arm of the cross reminds us of the Trinity. We are made children of the Triune God; Father, Son, and Holy Spirit, through our Baptism. *Matthew 28:19 - 20*

Ascension Lutheran Church
Danville, VA

Upright of Cross

1. Center one **8mm** pearl bead on the 18-inch 28 gauge wire.
2. Add one **8mm** pearl bead to each side and
3. crossover with one **6mm** pearl bead.
4. Add one **6mm** pearl bead to each side and
5. crossover with one **6mm** pearl bead.
6. Repeat 7 times
7. Add one **8mm** pearl bead to each side and
8. crossover with one **8mm** pearl bead.
9. Twist wires to make a hanger.

Crossbar of Cross

1. Center one **8mm** pearl bead on the second 18-inch 28 gauge wire.
2. Add one **8mm** pearl bead to each side
3. and crossover with one **6mm** pearl bead.
4. Add one **6mm** pearl bead to each side and
5. crossover with one 6mm pearl bead.
6. Repeat 2 times.
7. Thread the upper wire up into the 4th **6mm** bead from the top of the upright.
8. Thread the lower wire down through the 5th **6mm** bead from the top of the upright.
9. Thread the upper wire across the 4th **6mm** from the top of the upright.

10. Thread the lower wire across the 6th **6mm** bead from the top of the upright.
11. Thread the upper wire down through the 4th **6mm** bead on the opposite side of the upright.
12. Thread the lower wire up into the 5th **6mm** bead on the opposite side of the upright.
13. Crossover with 1 **6mm** bead.
14. Add one **6mm** bead to each wire
15. and crossover with one **6mm** bead.
16. Repeat 2 times.
17. Add one **8mm** pearl bead to each side and
18. crossover with one **8mm** pearl bead.
19. Secure wires by running each wire back weaving through the previous **8mm** bead and crossover in the next 6mm bead.

Chrismons™ Ornaments

Ascension Lutheran Church 314 West Main Street
Danville, Virginia 24540 Phone: 434-792-5795
Web: chrismon.org Facebook, Pinterest, Etsy
E-mail: chrismonsministry@gmail.com
Copyright 2016 Lutheran Church of the Ascension, Danville, VA

Difficulty: Advanced
Finished size: 6 inches
Beads:
93 3mm gold
76 4mm gold
103 5mm gold
50 6mm gold

18 3x6mm pearl
42 2mm pearl
245 3mm pearl
Wires:
26 - inch 28 gauge silver
  28 gauge gold wires
2 - 15"   2 - 23"
6 - 13"   1 - 30"

Chrismons
(CHRISt + MONogramS)

CELTIC CROSS

Latin Cross with Everlasting circle and Vine.

The Latin Cross: A reminder of our Lord's sacrifice.

The Circle: Always a symbol of our Lord's everlasting love. The original meaning may have been the sun, a welcome sign in a northern climate or a symbol of unity. It may also simple have been to hold up the heavy arms of the cross.

The Ornamentation: Elaborate carvings adorn many ancient Celtic Crosses. Basket weaves, medallions, serpents and vines. The vine here represents the true vine, rooted in the Trinity.

Ascension Lutheran Church
Danville, Virginia

Crossbar of Cross

Working from center of cross to the right then left creating the crossbar. See figure 2 page 14. *For these instructions "Both" refers to holding two wires ends together to add a bead and "Each" refers to separate wires.*

1. Center 12 **4mm** beads on the 20-inch 28 gauge wire.
2. Cross over the wire ends in the last circle bead joining the ends.
3. Center a 16" piece of 28 gauge wire in an adjoining bead on the circle.

4. String two **4mm** beads on both center wires out from the 12 bead circle.

5. String a **5mm** bead on each side wire.
6. Cross over one side and one center wire in a **4mm** bead.
7. Cross over the other side and center wire in a **4mm** bead.

8. Run a **4mm** bead over both center wires and string a **6mm** bead over each side wire.
9. Cross over each center and side wires with 2 **4mm** beads.

FIGURE 37

INDIVIDUAL SYMBOLS

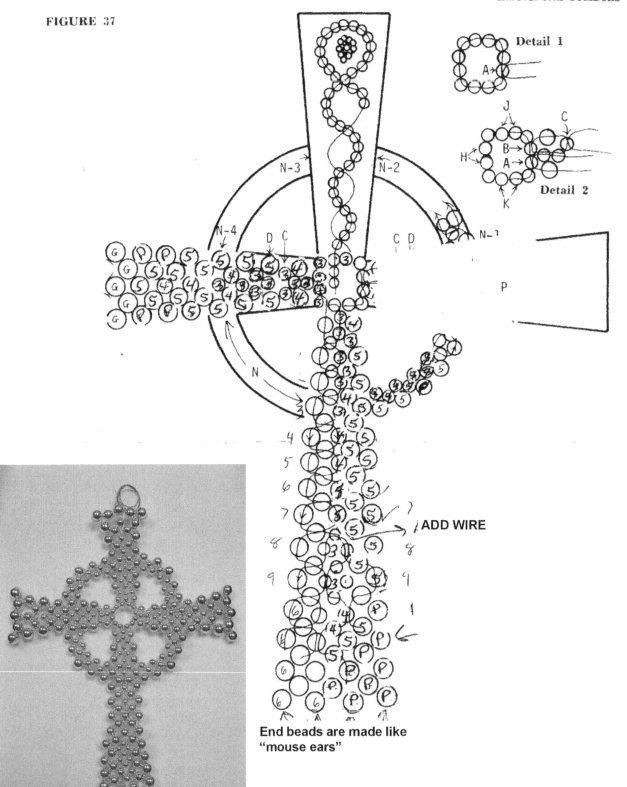

Detail 1

Detail 2

ADD WIRE

End beads are made like "mouse ears"

10. Run a **4mm** bead over both center wires and string a **6mm** bead over each side wire. Cross over each center and side wire with **5mm** bead.

11. Run a **4mm** bead over both center wires and string a **6mm** bead over each side wire. Cross over each center and side wire with a **6mm** bead.

12. Run a **5mm** bead over both center wires and string a **6mm** bead over each side wire. Cross over each center and side wire with a **6mm** bead.

13. Run a **4mm** bead over both center wires and string a **6mm** bead over each side wire. Cross over each center and side wire with a **6mm** bead.

14. Run a **6mm** bead over both center wires and string a **6mm** bead over each side wire. Cross over each center and side wire with a **6mm** bead.

15. Run a **6mm** bead over both center wires and string a 6mm bead over each side wire. Cross over each center and side wire with a **6mm** bead.

16. Run a **6mm** gold bead over both center wires and each side wire.

17. Back weave the wires from the center bead to anchor them.

18. Run the wire from the corner bead back through its adjacent bead. Position corner bead so that a little slack is in the wires into and out of bead. Hold the woven arm and the leftover wire in one hand, turn bead F with the other hand so that the wires twist on themselves to hold F in place.

19. Back weave the left leftover wire through a bead or two before cutting off the excess wire.

Second Arm

1. Insert a 16" length of 28 gauge wire through each of the two opposite beads on the twelve bead circle.

2. Repeat steps 4-19 above. Weave outward to make the right arm of the cross as the left was woven.

Top Extension

1. Insert a 24" length of 28 gauge wire through each of the two top beads on Detail 2, page 14.

2. Repeat steps 4-16 to create the top extension similar to the arms.

3. At the top, twist and back weave the wires from each corner bead.

4. Twist the wires from the center bead around each other atop to make the hanger.

Cross Leg

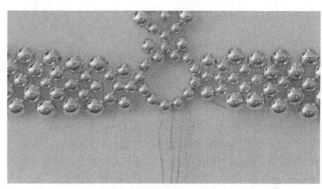

1. Insert a 24" length of 28 gauge wire through each of the two beads on Detail 2, page 14.

2. Run two **3mm** beads over both center wires. Add one **4mm** bead to each outside wire. Cross over with a **3mm** bead one center wire and one outside wire twice.

3. Run one **3mm** bead over both center wires.

Add one **5mm** bead to each side wire and cross over each center and side wire with a **3mm** bead.

4. Run one **3mm** bead over both center wires. Add one **5mm** bead to each side wire. Cross over each center and side wire with a 4mm bead.

5. Run one **3mm** bead over both center wires. Add one **5mm** bead to each side wire. Cross over each center and side wire with a **5mm** bead

6. Run one **4mm** bead over both center wires. Add one **5mm** bead to each side wire. Cross over each center and side wire with a **5mm** bead.

7. Run one **4mm** bead over both center wires. Add one **5mm** bead to each side wire. Cross over each center and side wire with a **5mm** bead.

8. Run one **4mm** bead over both center wires. Add one **5mm** bead to each side wire. Cross over each center and side wire with a **5mm** bead.

9. Run one **5mm** bead over both center wires. Add one **5mm** bead to each side wire. Cross over each center and side wire with a **5mm** bead.

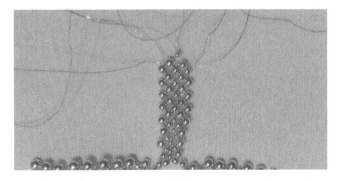

10. Run one **3mm** bead over both center wires. Add one 13" wire through the **3mm** bead. Add one **3mm** bead to both left side wires coming from center bead. Add one **3mm** bead to both right wires coming for the center **3mm** bead. Using two of the center wires, crossover in one **3mm** bead. Add one **5mm** bead to right and left side wire. Using the unused wire from center bead, and a side wire, cross over in a **5mm** bead. Do the same cross over on the opposite side. *This*

is where I begin calling the extra wire the "Middle" wire on each side. You may need to take a stiff paper or card board and cut notches at the top center, a few inches left and right, and on the side to hold your wires between steps.

11. Add one **3mm** bead to both Left middle and center wires. Add one **3mm** bead to both Right middle and center wires. Use center wires to crossover with one **3mm** bead. Add one **5mm** bead to left and right side wires. Cross over in one **5mm** bead using the middle and side wire. Repeat crossover on

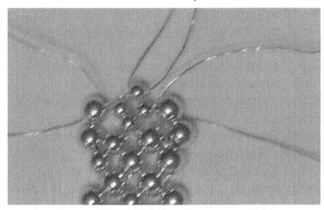

opposite side.

12. Add one **4mm** bead to both left center and middle wires and one **4mm** bead to both right center and middle wires. Separate wires using two center wires to cross over in one **4mm** bead. Add one **6mm** bead to left and right side wires. Use middle and side wire to cross over in one **5mm** bead. Repeat crossover on opposite side.

13. Add one **5mm** bead to both left center and middle wires and one **5mm** bead to both right center and middle wires. Separate wires and cross over in center wires using one **5mm** bead. Add one **6mm** bead to each left and right side wires. Use one side and middle wire to cross over in one **6mm** bead. Repeat crossover on opposite side.

14. Add one **6mm** bead to left middle and center wires. Add one **6mm** bead to right middle and center wires. Separate wires and use 2 center most wires to cross over in one **6mm** bead. Add one **6mm** bead to both far left and right side wires. Cross over with one **6mm** bead using left and middle wire. Re-

19. Return weave all wires and trim.

Nimbus
1. Add 28 in. wire in third **5mm** bead on outer edge of leg.
2. Add one **4mm** bead to inside wire and one **5mm** bead to outside wire. Crossover in one **4mm** bead.
3. Repeat step 2 three times.
4. Add one **4mm** bead to inside wire and one **5mm** bead to outside wire. Crossover in third **5mm** bead on the bottom of the cross arm to connect to arm.
5. Weave wires up through beads to the 3rd **5mm** bead on the top of the cross arm.
6. Repeat steps 2—4 until the nimbus is complete.

peat cross over on right side.

15. Add one **6mm** bead to left side wire. Run the wire from the corner bead back through its adjacent bead. Position corner bead so that a little slack is in the wires into and out of bead. Hold the woven arm and the leftover wire in one hand, turn bead with the other hand so that the wires twist on themselves to hold corner bead in place.
16. Repeat step 15 on right side.
17. Use one **6mm** bead and cross over using left middle and center wire.
18. Repeat crossover on right two middle and center wires.

Leaves

1. For Use 6 inch 28 gauge silver wire.
2. Center 1 **2mm** bead on 6 in. wire.
3. Add one **3x6** bead on each wire and cross over with 1 **2mm** bead.

4. On one wire add 1 **2mm** bead, 1 **3x6** bead, 1 **2mm** bead and 1 **3x6** bead.
5. Feed wire back through the first **2mm** bead on that same wire.
6. Repeat on the remaining wire.

7. To complete cluster, cross over in 1 **2mm** bead.
8. Repeat two times, for a total of 3 clusters.
9. Attach clusters to arms and top of cross as shown.

Vine

1. Thread 7 **2mm** seed beads on one end of wire and return weave end through the last 6 beads to burry end of

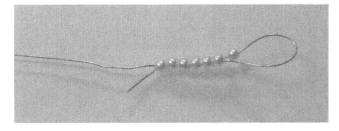

wire and secure work.
2. Repeat with 7 more **2mm** seed beads on remaining wire.
3. Feed all **3mm** pearls from string onto the wire.
4. Feed 7 **2mm** seed beads one end of wire and return weave to secure work.
5. Attach one end of wire at base of gold cross.
6. Lay vine on top of cross in a free-form design. Edges of vine should reach the edge of the outer edge of the circle next to the leaves.
7. Secure vine to cross with gold wire as needed.

Vine Option 2 (requires more than 245 **3mm** pearls)

1. Center one **3mm** pearl on center of 30 in. silver wire and attach center at the base of the top leaf cluster.
2. Feed up to 7 **3mm** beads on each wire and cross over in one **3mm** bead.
3. Run one wire through the cross front to back then back to front to attach vine.
4. Repeat steps 2 & 3 until you reach the base of the cross.
5. Thread 7 **2mm** seed beads on one end of wire and return weave end through the last 6 beads to secure.
6. Repeat twice with 7 more **2mm** seed beads to create 3 tails at the end of the vine.
7. Using a shorter silver wire, center the wire in one **3mm** pearl bead on the left side of the vine crossing the center of the cross.
8. Repeat steps 2 and 3 until your reach the leaf cluster and attach the last vine loop under the leaf cluster.
9. Repeat steps 7 and 8 for right cross arm vine.

Chrismons™ Ornaments

Ascension Lutheran Church 314 West Main Street
Danville, Virginia 24540 Phone: 434-792-5795
Web: chrismon.org Facebook, Pinterest, Etsy
E-mail: chrismonsministry@gmail.com

XP
Chi Rho

Difficulty: Beginner

Finished size: 3.5 inches

Beads:

113 - 5mm gold beads

Wire:

2 16 - inch 28 gauge gold

1 20 - inch 26 gauge gold

Chrismons

(CHRISt + MONogramS)

XP
Chi Rho

The first letters of Christ (CHR) in the Greek Alphabe. XPIOTOS or Christos

Or

The initials for Christ the King in Latin Christus Rex

Most of the monograms of Christ Jesus are based on Greek words. The first two letters, Chi and Rho are superimposed on each other, to create this Chrismons.

Ascension Lutheran Church
Danville, VA

Chi Rho - Instructions may be used to create a 5mm or 6mm version of this pattern.

Chi - X

1. Place 2 beads on one 16-inch 28ga wire. CC with one bead.
2. Add one bead to each side, CC with one bead. Repeat 10 times.
3. Add two beads and back weave to secure the wire. *(You will have 12 center beads)*
4. Place 2 beads on second 16-inch 28ga wire. CC with one bead.
5. Add one bead to each side CC with one bead. Repeat 3 times.
6. Add one bead to upper wire. Thread two wires into first leg of X at the 6th and 7th bead.
7. Add one bead to the bottom wire. CC with one bead.
8. Add one bead to each side CC with one bead. Repeat 4 times.
9. Add two beads and back weave to secure the wire. *(You will have 5 center beads on each leg of the X)*

RHO - P

1. Center 1 bead on the 20-inch 26ga wire.
2. Add one bead to one side return the wire thru the center bead.
3. Add one bead to the other side return the wire thru the center bead.

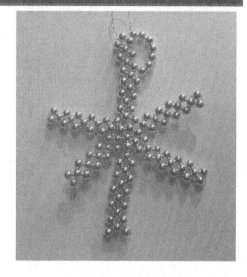

4. Add one bead to each side and CC with one bead. Repeat 4 times.
5. Weave thru center of Chi - X to attach.
6. CC with one bead.
7. Add one bead to each side and CC with one bead. Repeat 5 times.
8. Return weave left wire thru center bead and right bead.
9. Holding two wires together, add 7 beads to the wire.
10. Thread both wires thru the 4th bead from the top of the P.
11. Separate the wires and return weave to secure.

Chi Rho with Alpha Omega

After completing your Chi Rho, follow directions for making the letters Alpha and Omega shown on pages 43 & 44 of this book.

Attach from the third bead from the bottom row of the top arms of the Chi.

Chrismons™ Ornaments

Ascension Lutheran Church 314 West Main Street
Danville, Virginia 24540 Phone: 434-792-5795
Web: chrismon.org Facebook, Pinterest, Etsy
E-mail: chrismonsministry@gmail.com
Copyright 2014 Lutheran Church of the Ascension, Danville, VA

XP
Chi Rho in Eternity

Difficulty: Intermediate

Finished size: 4 inches

Beads:
37 - 5x7mm gold
37 - 5mm gold
37 - 6mm gold
84 - 3mm pearl
24 - 4mm pearl
26 - 5mm pearl

Wire:
1 55 - inch 28 gauge gold
2 16 - inch 28 gauge silver
1 20 - inch 28gauge gold

Chrismons

(CHRISt + MONogramS)

XP

Chi Rho

The first letters of Christ (CHR) in the Greek Alphabet. XPICTOC or Christos

Or

The initials for Christ the King in Latin Christus Rex

Christ wrapped in a never ending circle, representing God's everlasting love.

Ascension Lutheran Church
Danville, VA

Everlasting XP Chi Rho

The first letters of Christ (CHR) in the Greek Alphabet. XPIOTOS or Christos. Or, the initials for Christ the King in the Latin Christus Rex. Christ wrapped in a never ending circle, representing God's everlasting love.

Circle
1. Center one 5x7 gold bead on 55 - inch 28-gauge gold wire.
2. Add one **5mm** and one **6mm** on each side.
3. CC with one 5x7 gold bead.
4. Repeat until you have used 37 5x7 beads, keeping all **5mm** beads on the inside and **6mm** beads on the outside.
5. Close circle in **first** 5x7 bead and create hanger.

RHO - P
1. Center 20-inch silver wire to bottom 5mm gold bead. (this will be the 20th bead from the top including the hanger bead.)
2. Add one **5mm** pearl bead to each side and CC with one **5mm** pearl
3. Add one **3mm** bead to each side and CC with one **5mm** bead.
4. Repeat 12 times. You will have 14 center **5mm** beads.
5. Add one **5mm** to left side of P. Return weave left wire thru top center 5mm gold bead
6. CC both wire in one **5mm** pearl bead.
7. Return weave left wire thru top center **5mm** gold bead. CC both wire in one **5mm** pearl bead.
8. Holding two wires together, add 7 beads to the wire.
9. Thread both wires thru the 5th center **4mm** bead counting down from the top of the P.

10. Separate the wires and return weave to secure.

Chi - X
1. Center one 16-inch silver wire on the sixth gold bead from the bottom of the P.
2. (do not count the bottom bead).
3. Add one **3mm** pearl bead to each side, CC with one **4mm** pearl bead. Repeat 5 times.
4. Add one **3mm** pearl to each wire CC with one 3mm pearl.
5. Using outside wire weave through the 7th from the bottom **3mm** pearl on the P. CC in one **3mm** pearl.
6. Using inside wire back weave through last outer **3mm** pearl of 1st leg of X.
7. Add one **3mm** pearl to outside wire, CC in one **4mm** pearl.
8. Add one **3mm** pearl to each wire and CC with one **4mm** pearl. Repeat 4 times.
9. (you will have 6 **4mm** pearls on each leg of X)
10. Add one **3mm** pearl to each side and weave into circle at 6th gold bead from where you attached the wire.
11. Repeat on other side of P. Always count from bottom of P.

Ascension Lutheran Church 314 West Main Street
Danville, Virginia 24540 Phone: 434-792-5795
Web: chrismon.org Facebook, Pinterest, Etsy
E-mail: chrismonsministry@gmail.com
Copyright 2016 Lutheran Church of the Ascension, Danville, VA

Difficulty: Intermediate

Finished size: 4 inches

Supplies:
  Pearl, Gold, or clear seed
    beads
1 3x6mm pearl
1 4 inch diameter wood
    base painted gold
1 White Rose (Paint
    leaves gold)
3/16 inch diameter wood
    dowel painted gold cut
    to 4 inches
Gold Paint
Heavy flexible clear plastic
    for Butterfly base
    (Shower Curtain Liner)

Chrismons

(CHRISt + MONogramS)

50th Anniversary Cross 1957 - 2006

The Latin cross a reminder of
our Lord's sacrifice for our sins,
by which we receive forgiveness
and salvation.

Ascension Lutheran Church
Danville, VA

Chrismons 50th Anniversary Cross 1957 - 2006

Designed by
Robert Shaver
Constructed by
Martha Gray McCauley

1. Begin by making the Jesus Cross on page 43 without inserting center beads.
2. Prepare a small hole 1/2 inch deep in the base to fit the 3/16 inch dowel
3. Cut dowel to 4 inches and insert in base securing with wood clue.
4. Separate leaves from rose.
5. Paint base, dowel and leaves gold.
6. Size butterfly pattern to fit proportions of cross and cut out of plastic.
7. Punch tiny holes to sew bead details of butterfly and the Alpha and Omega. Fill in with pearl or clear beads.
8. Assemble ornament by securing leaves to base.
9. Feed rose over dowel rod and glue to the base.
10. Feed Cross over dowel rod and secure with glue.
11. Attach butterfly to cross.

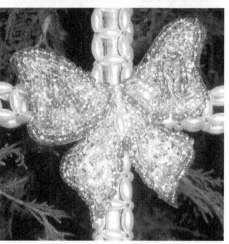

Permission is granted to photo copy and resize the above sketch for personal use.

Chrismons™ Ornaments

Ascension Lutheran Church 314 West Main Street
Danville, Virginia 24540 Phone: 434-792-5795
Web: chrismon.org Facebook, Pinterest, Etsy
E-mail: chrismonsministry@gmail.com
Copyright 2014 Lutheran Church of the Ascension, Danville, VA

Chrismons 50th Anniversary Gift Cross

Difficulty: Beginner

Finished size: 3.25 inches

Beads:

49   6mm gold or pearl

Wires:

14 - inch 28 gauge wire

12 - inch 28 gauge wire

Use gold wire with gold beads or silver wire with pearls beads.

Chrismons

(CHRISt + MONogramS)

50th Anniversary Gift Cross

1957 - 2006

The Latin cross a reminder of our Lord's sacrifice for our sins, by which we receive forgiveness and salvation.

Given as a gift to the congregation in remembrance of the 50th Anniversary of the Chrismons Ministry.

Ascension Lutheran Church
Danville, VA

Upright of Cross

1. Center three **6mm** beads on the 14-inch 28 gauge wire.
2. Crossover with one **6mm** bead.
3. Add one **6mm** bead to each wire.
4. Crossover with one **6mm** bead.
5. Repeat until you have 10 center beads.
6. Add one **6mm** bead to each wire.
7. Crossover with one **6mm** bead.
8. Twist the two wires to create a hanger.

Arms of Cross

1. Center three **6mm** beads on the 12-inch 28 gauge wire.
2. Crossover with one **6mm** bead.
3. Add one **6mm** bead to each wire.
4. Crossover with one **6mm** bead.
5. Add one **6mm** bead to each wire.

6. Thread the two wires through the 3rd and 4th center beads from the top of the upright.
7. Add one **6mm** bead to each wire.
8. Crossover with one **6mm** bead.
9. Repeat once.
10. Add one **6mm** bead to each wire.
11. Crossover with one **6mm** bead.
12. Back weave until secure.
13. Cut wires.

Ascension Lutheran Church 314 West Main Street
Danville, Virginia 24540 Phone: 434-792-5795
Web: chrismon.org Facebook, Pinterest, Etsy
E-mail: chrismonsministry@gmail.com
Copyright 2016 Lutheran Church of the Ascension, Danville, VA

Difficulty: Advanced
Finished size: 3 inches

Crown Supplies
Beads:
 96 3mm pearl
120 3mm gold
 24 3x6mm gold
Wire:
1 24-inch 28 gauge silver
2 24-inch 28 gauge gold

Cross Supplies
Beads:
 140 3x6mm pearl
 17 6mm gold
Wire:
4 16-inch 28 gauge silver
4 20-inch 28 gauge silver

Chrismons

(CHRISt + MONogramS)

Christ the King Cross and Crown

The Latin cross a reminder of our Lord's sacrifice for our sins, by which we receive forgiveness and salvation.

The Crown reminds of us the Kingship of our Lord, Jesus Christ, The **King** of Kings and **Lord** of lords.

1 Timothy 6:15

Ascension Lutheran Church
Danville, VA

12 point Crown

Base circle for Crown
1. Fold 24 inch wire in half.
2. Center one **3mm** pearl on wire.
3. Add one **3mm** pearl bead to right side of wire and one **4mm** gold bead to left side of wire.
4. Crossover with one **3mm** pearl bead. *The gold beads will always be on the same side.*

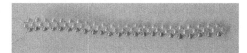

5. Add one **3mm** pearl bead to right side of wire and one **3mm** gold bead to left side of wire.
6. Crossover with one **3mm** pearl bead.
7. Repeat until you have 24 center beads.
8. Add one **3mm** pearl bead to right side of wire and one **3mm** gold bead to left side of wire.
9. Crossover in first pearl bead to form a ring.
10. Continue weaving to next crossover to secure wires.
11. Cut wires.

Lower band
1. Center one 24 inch gold wire in one gold bead on base circle.
2. Add one pearl and one gold bead to each wire
3. Crossover in two **3mm** pearls
4. ADD: 1g 2p 1g 1p
5. Return weave thru 2nd gold

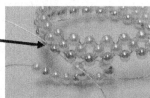

6. Add 1 pearl
7. Return weave down one gold
8. Return weave thru 2 pearl beads

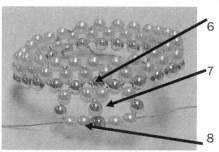

6
7
8

9. Repeat steps 4 - 8 around the band.

10. Add one 3mm gold to each wire and Crossover in two 3mm pearls to complete circle. Back weave wire near side with two pearls above gold.
11. Feed other wire up through original gold bead, add 3mm pearl and back weave to complete lower band of crown.

Upper Points
Use one 24 inch gold 28-gauge wire

1. Center wire on one pearl bead on base circle
2. On one wire add 2 **3mm** gold beads, 1 **3x6mm**, 3 **3mm** gold, 1 **3x6mm**. *This becomes your upper wire.*
3. *Lower wire* add 1 **3mm** gold
4. Crossover in 1 **3mm** gold
5. Upper: 1 **3x6mm** , 3 **3mm** gold, 1 **3x6mm**
6. Lower: 1 round, weave through 2ⁿᵈ pearl, 1 round
7. Crossover in 1 **3mm** gold

8. On previous loop twist the three 3mm gold beads to form point.

9. Repeat steps 5 - 8 all the way around.
10. Final point repeat steps 5 and 6 crossing over in second gold bead to connect the upper band.
11. Twist remaining points and back weave to secure wires.

Jesus Cross with 11 center beads

Upright of Cross

1. Fold first 20-inch wire in half.
2. Place three **3x6mm** beads on first wire.
3. Crossover with one **3x6mm** bead
4. Repeat with second 20-inch wire.
5. Fold third 20-inch wire in half .
6. Place one **3x6mm** beads on third wire.
7. Thread one side of third wire into one side bead of the first wire.
8. Thread other side of third wire into one side bead of the second wire.

9. Crossover with one **3x6mm** bead.
10. Fold fourth 20-inch wire in half .
11. Place one **3x6mm** bead on fourth wire.
12. Thread one side of fourth wire into the remaining side bead of the first wire and the other side of the fourth wire into the remaining side bead of the second wire.
13. Crossover with one **3x6mm** bead.
14. Insert one 6mm bead into the box and pull all wires tight.
15. At this point you will have eight wires above 3 rows of 4 concentric beads.
16. Add four beads, one to each corner of double wires.
17. Crossover four beads using one wire from each corner.
18. Insert one 6mm bead into the box and pull all wires tight.
19. Repeat until you have 11 boxes with 11 beads inside.
20. To end, return weave one wire from each corner. Use remaining four wires to create a hanger.

Arms of Cross
1. Fold first 16-inch wire in half.
2. Place three **3x6mm** beads on first wire.
3. Crossover with one **3x6mm** bead.
4. Repeat with second 16-inch wire.
5. Fold third 16-inch wire in half .
6. Place one **3x6mm** beads on third wire.
7. Thread one side of third wire into one side bead of the first wire.
8. Thread other side of third wire into one side bead of the second wire.
9. Crossover with one **3x6mm** bead.
10. Fold fourth 16-inch wire in half .
11. Place one **3x6mm** bead on fourth wire.
12. Thread one side of fourth wire into the remaining side bead of the first wire and the other side of the fourth wire into the remaining side bead of the second wire.
13. Crossover with one **3x6mm** bead.
14. Insert one **6mm** bead into box, pull all wires tight.
15. At this point you will have eight wires above one box.
16. Add four beads, one to each corner of double wires.
17. Crossover four beads using one wire from each corner.
18. Insert one **6mm** bead into box, pull all wires tight.
19. Repeat for second box.
20. Add four beads, one to each corner of double wires.
21. Weave double corner wires through 4ᵗʰ and 5ᵗʰ **3x6** beads on each side of the upright.
22. Insert an **6mm** bead and pull cross arm tight to upright.
23. Add four beads, one to each corner of double wires.
24. Crossover four beads using one wire from each corner.
25. Insert one **6mm** bead into box, pull all wires tight.
26. Repeat until you have 3 boxes on this side of the upright.
27. To end, return weave all wires.

Ascension Lutheran Church 314 West Main Street
Danville, Virginia 24540 Phone: 434-792-5795
Web: chrismon.org Facebook, Pinterest, Etsy
E-mail: chrismonsministry@gmail.com
Copyright 2016 Lutheran Church of the Ascension, Danville, VA

Difficulty: Advanced
Finished size: 4 inches
Beads:

113 3mm pearl
32 3x6mm pearl
1 6mm pearl
16 3mm gold
245 4mm gold
76 3x6mm gold

Wire:

3 ft - 28 gauge Silver
2 12 - inch 26 gauge gold
5-1/2 ft - 26 gauge gold

Chrismons

(CHRISt + MONogramS)

Christ's Monograms

The initials and abbreviations of Christ are incorporated within the center design of the cross.

*The first letters of Christ (CHR) in the Greek Alphabet **XPIOTOS** or Christos Chi Rho (XP or XPC)*

IC or IS and The initials for Christ the King in Latin Christus Rex

Ascension Lutheran Church
Danville, VA

White center.   3 ft wire.

1. Center one **3mm** pearl on 3 ft. wire. This bead is "A".
2. Add a **3x6mm** to each wire. Crossover with one **3mm** pearl
3. "Lopsided corner" Add 1 **3mm** pearl to outside wire. Cross over with 1 **3mm** pearl.
4. Add a **3x6mm** pearl to each wire. Crossover with 1 **3mm** pearl.
5. Add a **3mm** pearl to each wire. Crossover with 1 **3mm** pearl.
6. Repeat steps 2 - 5, 6 more times.
7. Connect top of circle. Add 1 **3mm** pearl to each wire.
8. Thread top wire down through first bead (A).
9. Use same wire to crossover in bottom pearl. Pull tight.
10. Add 1 **3mm** pearl to each wire. Crossover with a **3mm** pearl.
11. Repeat 3 times.
12. Add a **3mm** bead to each wire. Crossover in a **6mm** bead.
13. Add a **3mm** bead to each wire.
14. Add 1 **3mm** bead to each wire. Crossover with a **3mm** pearl.
15. Repeat 2 times.
16. Crossover in center inside **3mm** pearl on opposite side.
17. Weaves wires through circle and

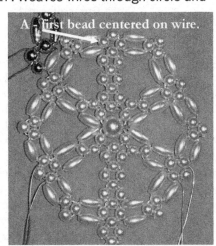

A - first bead centered on wire.

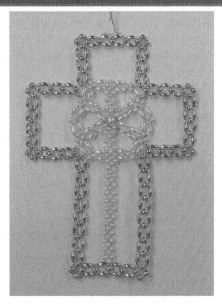

cross over in center **3mm** pearl.
18. Add 1 **3mm** pearl to each wire. Cross over in a **3mm** pearl.
19. Repeat 12 more times.

Inner circle - Legs of Chi

2 - 1 ft wires

1. Thread wire through inside bead of 4 bead cluster.
2. Add 1 **3x6mm** bead to each wire. Crossover in 1 **3mm** bead.
3. Add 3mm to short side wire and thread down through last **3mm** side bead before **6mm** bead.
4. Add **3x6mm** pearl to long side wire.
5. Thread both wires through center **6mm** bead.
6. Thread 1 wire through **3mm** bead next to **6mm** bead and add **3x6** pearl to remaining wire. Crossover in 1 **3mm** pearl.

7. Add 1 **3x6** bead to each wire.
8. Crossover in **3mm** bead of 4 - bead cluster.

Gold Cross   5 ½ ft wire

1. Center **4mm** gold bead on 5 1/2 ft. gold wire. Add 1 **4mm** gold to each wire and crossover in **4mm** gold.
2. Add 1 **3x6** gold to each wire. Crossover in 1 **4mm** bead.
3. Repeat 3 more times.
4. Corner: Add 2 - **4mm** gold to one wire. Crossover in a **4mm** gold. Wires should now be at a 90° angle forming the corner of the cross.
5. Add 1 **3x6mm** gold to each wire and crossover in a **4mm** bead.
6. Repeat 2 times.
7. Attach pearl circle: Run inner wire through **3x6** pearl.
8. Add 1 **3mm** gold to same wire. Crossover in a **4mm** gold.
9. Add 1 **3x6mm** gold bead to each wire. Crossover in 1 **4mm** bead.
10. Repeat 2 times.
11. Corner: Add 2 **4mm** gold to outside wire. Crossover in a **4mm** gold. Wires should now be at a 90° angle.
12. Add 1 **3x6** gold to each wire. Cross over in 1 **4mm** gold.
13. Repeat 3 times.
14. Corner: Add 2 **4mm** gold to outside wire crossover in a **4mm** gold bead.
15. Add 1 **3x6** to each wire. Crossover in a **4mm** gold.
16. Repeat 2 times.
17. Add 1 - **3mm** gold to top wire and thread through **3x6** pearl on pearl circle.
18. Crossover in 1 **4mm** gold.
19. Add 1 **3x6** gold to each wire. Crossover in 1 **4mm** bead.
20. Repeat 7 times.
21. Add 2 **4mm** gold to outside wire. Crossover in a **4mm** bead.
22. Add 1 **3x6mm** gold to each wire. Crossover in 1 **4mm** gold. Repeat.
23. Thread nearest silver wire from bottom of white cross back through inside gold **3x6** and down through **4mm** bead.
24. Thread remaining silver wire and gold wire into gold **3x6mm** and 1 **3x6mm** to bottom wire. Keeping silver wire with the gold, crossover in 1 **4mm** bead. Cut silver wires.
25. Add 1 **3x6mm** to each wire and crossover in 1 **4mm** bead.

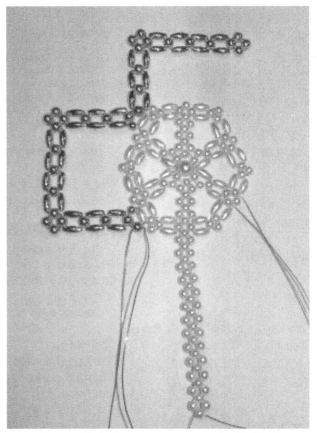

26. Corner: Add 2 **4mm** beads to outside wire. Crossover in 1 **4mm** bead.
27. Add 1 **3x6mm** to each wire and crossover in 1 4mm bead.
28. Repeat 7 times.
29. Thread inside wire through white 3x6mm on circle. Add 1 **3mm** bead to same wire. Crossover in 1 **4mm** gold.
30. Add 1 **3x6** gold to each wire and crossover in **14mm** gold.
31. Repeat 2 more times.
32. Corner: Add 2 **4mm** beads to outside wire. Crossover in 1 **4mm** bead.
33. Add 1 **3x6** to each wire. Crossover in 1 **4mm** bead. Repeat 3 times.
34. Corner: Add 2 **4mm** gold to outside wire. Crossover in 1 **4mm** gold.
35. Add 1 **3x6mm** to each wire. Crossover in 1 **4mm** gold. Repeat 2 times.
36. Add 1 3mm gold to inside wire and thread through white **3x6** on circle. Crossover in 1 **4mm** bead.
37. Add 1 **3x6** to each wire. Crossover in 1 **4mm** bead. Repeat 1 time.
38. Add 1 **3x6** to each wire and crossover in bottom **4mm** bead of first corner cluster.
39. Back weave to secure ends.

Chrismons™ Ornaments

Ascension Lutheran Church 314 West Main Street
Danville, Virginia 24540 Phone: 434-792-5795
Web: chrismon.org Facebook, Pinterest, Etsy
E-mail: chrismonsministry@gmail.com
Copyright 2016 Lutheran Church of the Ascension, Danville, VA

Cross in Gloria

Difficulty: Intermediate

Finished size: 4.75 inches

Beads:

46 5mm pearl

26 6mm pearl

36 2mm gold

44 3mm gold

20 4mm gold

36 3x6 gold

Wires:

1 18-inch 28 gauge silver

1 21-inch 28 gauge silver

2 24-inch 28 gauge gold

1 18-inch 28 gauge gold

Cross in Gloria

*The rising sun behind the Cross
suggests a new day
when our Lord
conquered death for us.*

*Cross
with Nimbus and Rays*

Latin Cross: A reminder of our
Lord's sacrifice.

Nimbus: A circle of light around
the head that connotes Godliness
or holiness.

Rays: Light - "I am the light of
the world" John 8:12

*Ascension Lutheran Church
Danville, Virginia*

John 8:2

2 At dawn he appeared again in the temple courts, where all the people gathered around him, and he sat down to teach them. NIV

Cross Upright

1. Place one **6mm** pearl bead on 21-inch silver wire. Add one **5mm** pearl bead to each side, crossover with 1 **6mm** pearl bead.
2. Add one **5mm** bead to each side, crossover with one **6mm** bead.   Repeat 13 times.
3. Twist wires together for hanger.

Crossbar

1. Place one **6mm** bead on 18-inch silver wire. Add one **5mm** bead to each side, crossover with 1 **6mm** bead.
2. Add one **5mm** bead to each side, crossover with one **6mm** bead.   Repeat 2 times.
3. Join crossbar to upright
4. Weave upper wire up into the 5th **5mm** bead from the top of the upright. Weave the same wire through the 5th from the top **6mm** bead and weave the same wire down through the 5th from the top **5mm** bead on the opposite side of the upright.
5. Repeat with the lower wire.
6. Weave lower wire down into the 6th **5mm** bead from the top of the upright. Weave the same wire through the 7th from the top **6mm** bead and weave the same wire up through the 6th from the top **5mm** bead on the opposite side of the upright.
7. Add one **6mm** bead and crossover.
8. Add one **5mm** bead to each wire and crossover with

9. one **6mm** bead.

10. Repeat 3 times.

11. Secure the wires by back-weaving through one **5mm** and one **6mm** bead.

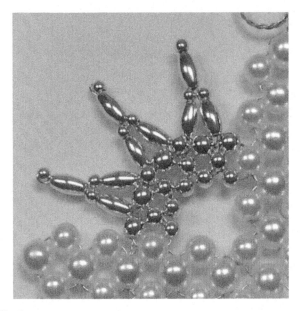

Nimbus

1. Insert 18-inch gold wire halfway into the upper third from the end **5mm** pearl on the right of the crossbar.

2. Add 1 **3mm** gold bead to the inner wire and 1 4mm gold bead to the outer wire.

3. Crossover with 1 **3mm** gold bead. Repeat 3 times.

4. Add 1 **3mm** gold bead to the inner wire and 1 **4mm** gold bead to the outer wire, crossover in the right-hand side third **5mm** pearl from the top of the upright.

5. Weave wires through the third and fourth **6mm** pearl bead from the top and crossover in the third from the top **5mm** bead on the opposite side of the upright.

Repeat for all four quadrants of the cross. *You will have 5 - 4mm beads in each quadrant of the cross.* Secure wires.

Rays

1. Add a 24-inch wire at the third 6mm pearl from the each off a crossbar.

2. Thread wire through two 4mm beads of the nimbus.

3. Add one **3x6mm** gold bead, one **2mm** gold bead, another **3x6mm** gold bead and another 2mm gold bead. Return weave through the second **3x6mm** bead, add a 2mm gold bead and a **3x6mm** gold bead, cross over in the second 4mm bead. Carefully pull the wire tight.

4. Add one **3mm** bead. Thread wire through next 4mm bead.

5. Add one **3x6mm** gold bead, one 2mm gold bead, another **3x6mm** gold bead and another 2mm gold bead. Return weave through the second **3x6mm** bead, add a **2mm** gold bead and a **3x6mm** gold bead, cross over in the 4mm bead. Carefully pull the wire tight.

6. Add one **3mm** bead. Thread wire through next 4mm bead.

7. Add one **3x6mm** gold bead, one **2mm** gold bead, another 3x6mm gold bead and another 2mm gold bead. Return weave through the second **3x6mm** bead, add a **2mm** gold bead and a **3x6mm** gold bead, cross over in the 4mm bead. Carefully pull the wire tight.

8. Thread wire through last **4mm** bead and through white cross at third from end **6mm** pearl.

9. Repeat for each quadrant. Add wire if needed.

10. Secure wire.

Chrismons™ Ornaments

✝

Ascension Lutheran Church 314 West Main Street
Danville, Virginia 24540 Phone: 434-792-5795
Web: chrismon.org Facebook, Pinterest, Etsy
E-mail: chrismonsministry@gmail.com
Copyright 2016 Lutheran Church of the Ascension, Danville, VA

Cross of Constantine

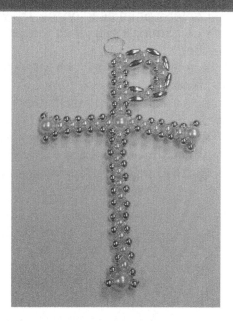

Difficulty: Advanced Beginner
Finished size: 3.75 inches
Beads:
  4 - 6mm pearl
  3 - 4mm pearl
 31- 3mm pearl
64 - 3mm gold
  8 - 3x6mm gold
Wire:
1 18 - inch 28 gauge silver
1 15 - inch 28 gauge gold
1 12 - inch 28 gauge silver

Chrismons

(CHRISt + MONogramS)

Cross of Constantine

The Chi Rho is part of the legend of how Constantine became the first Roman emperor to embrace Christianity. During a definitive battle for the city of Rome Constantine saw a sign in the sky with the words,

"In this sign conquer."

Whether the sign he saw was the cross or the Greek abbreviation for Christ is unknown. But it is certain that, after that military campaign was successfully concluded, he placed the Chi Rho symbol on his labarum or imperial standard. Thus the Chi Rho became associated with triumph. In addition to the original Greek meaning, a Latin interpretation was given to the letters – *Christus Rex* or Christ, the King

Ascension Lutheran Church
Danville, VA

Upright:

STARTING UPRIGHT

1. Form a hanger eye in the 18" wire. Cross-connect (CC) a **3mm** pearl.
2. Put a **3mm** gold on one wire and a **3mm** pearl on the other wire and a CC a **3mm** pearl.
3. Put a **3mm** gold on each wire and CC a **3mm** pearl.
4. Repeat one time.
5. Put a **3mm** gold on the same side as the last **3mm** gold and a **3mm** pearl on the same side as the 1st **3mm** pearl and CC a **3mm** pearl.
6. Put a **3mm** gold on each wire and CC with a **3mm** pearl.
7. Put a **3mm** gold on each wire and CC a **6mm** pearl.
8. Put a **3mm** gold on each wire and CC a **3mm** pearl.
9. Repeat the above step (9) more times.
10. Put a **3mm** gold on each wire and CC a **4mm** pearl.
11. Put a **3mm** gold on each wire and CC a **6mm** pearl.
12. Put a **3mm** gold on each wire and thread the wires back thru the **6mm** pearl.
13. Trim wires.

STARTING BOW OF RHO

Bow of RHO:
1. Thread the 12" wire per diagram to start bow.
2. Put a **3x6mm** gold on each wire and CC a **3mm** pearl.
3. Put a **3x6mm** gold on the outside wire, a **3mm** gold on the inside wire and CC a **3mm** pearl.
4. Repeat the above step three (3) more times.
5. Put a **3x6mm** gold on each wire and CC thru the 2nd **3mm** pearl on the side.
6. Thread the wires thru the upright per ending diagram and trim wires.

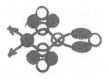

ENDING BOW OF RHO

29

Crossarm:

1. Center a **6mm** pearl on the 15" wire.
2. Put a **3mm** gold on each wire and CC a **4mm** pearl.
3. Put a **3mm** gold on each wire and CC a **4mm** pearl.
4. Put a **3mm** gold on each wire and CC a **3mm** pearl.
5. Repeat above step three (3) more times.
6. Attach the cross arm at the 6mm pearl below the RHO bow.

FIGURE 50

ATTACHING CROSSARM

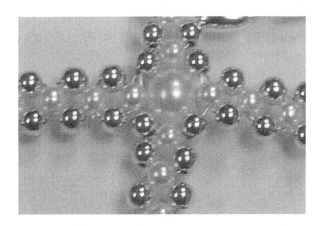

7. CC a **3mm** pearl on the other side of the upright.
8. Put a **3mm** gold on each wire and CC a **3mm** pearl.
9. Repeat the above step two (2) more times.
10. Put a **3mm** gold on each wire and CC a **4mm** pearl.
11. Put a **3mm** gold on each wire and CC a **6mm** pearl.
12. Put a **3mm** gold on each wire and thread back thru 6mm peal and trim wires.

Submitted by: Frank Graham Pritchard previously published in Chrismons Basic Series.

Chrismons™ Ornaments

Ascension Lutheran Church 314 West Main Street
Danville, Virginia 24540 Phone: 434-792-5795
Web: chrismon.org   Facebook, Pinterest, Etsy
E-mail: chrismonsministry@gmail.com

Difficulty: Intermediate

Finished size: Varries

Beads:
 1 gold ornament 2.5 inch
  diameter or 4 inch
  diameter
7—11 3mm pearls
100 4mm pearls (approx.)
80 3x6mm pearl (approx.)
Note: pattern may also be
  worked in 4mm and
  5mm pearls for 4 inch
  base.

Wire:
36 - inch + 3 x ball circumference in 28 gauge
  silver or 6 - foot will fit
  any ball

Chrismons
(CHRISt + MONogramS)

Cross Triumphant

A cross supreme over the
world symbolizes the
triumph of the Savior over
the sin of the world.

The world united in Christ
who has dominion over all.

Ascension Lutheran Church
Danville, VA

The Cross Triumphant is not diffi-
cult however this design requires
flexibility from the artist. The wrap
created around the ornament
must be tight and requires adjust-
ment to the design as you work.

Diagrams shown can also be found in
Chrismons Basic Series pages 49 and 50.

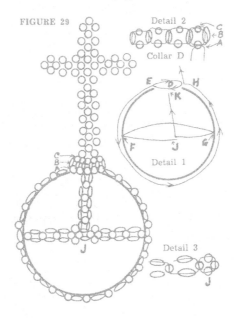

Collar
1. Center 1 3x6 pearl on wire.
2. Add 1 3mm pearl to one wire
   making that the top of the collar and 1 4mm pearl to other
   wire making that the bottom of
   the collar.
3. Cross over in 1 3x6 pearl
4. Repeat steps 2
   and 3 keeping
   3mm beads on
   top and 4mm
   beads on bottom
   until collar fits
   your ornament

base perfectly. (Detail 2 at
left) Close collar by adding one
more 3mm and 4mm pearls
top and bottom then cross
over in the
first 3x6 pearl.

5. Feed upper
   wire through
   the next 3mm
   bead and
   down through
   the 3x6mm

   pearl to the bottom through
   the 4mm bead so one wire ex-
   tends on each side of one
   4mm pearl. This bead is now
   position "H" in diagram

Note: The collar will take 7—11 beads
based on your ornament base. Most of
the pattern will be worked without the
ornament in place, but you will use the
ornament to measure your work to fit.

Circumference Wrap

1. Match the number of 4mm collar beads to figure 30 below and mark location of beads. "H" is the bead with wires on each side.

2. Add 1 **3x6** pearl to each wire and cross over with 1 **4mm** pearl. *See detail 3 on previous page.*

FIGURE 30   Row A Collar Beads

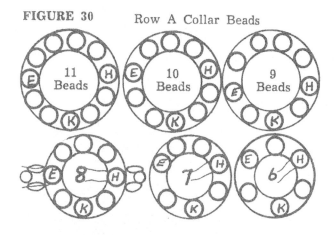

3. Repeat step 2 until the strand can circle the ornament and connect with a crossover in pearl **E** on the opposite side of the collar in **Figure 30** above.

4. Feed wires through 4mm beads back to H ending with one wire on each side of H fed up through a 3x6 bead toward the top of the collar.

5. Put wires aside for later.

Horizontal wrap

1. Center 1 **4mm** pearl on a 36 inch **28 gauge** wire.

2. Add 1 **4mm** pearl on each wire and cross over with 1 **4mm** pearl.

3. Add 1 **3x6 pearl** on each wire and cross over with 1 **4mm** pearl.

4. Repeat until one half of the front wrap is complete.

5. Cross over in F Side center bead as shown

on **Detail 2.**

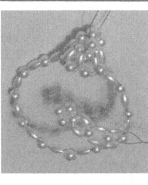

6. Continue pattern adding 1 **3x6** to each wire and crossing over in a **4mm** pearl adjusting pattern to fit ornament tight. Cross over in position **G** of *Figure 29* on previous page.

7. Insert ornament and continue pattern by adding 1 **3x6** pearl to each wire and crossing over in a **4mm** pearl.

8. When you are close to connecting to the beginning 4 bead cluster, add 1 **4mm** bead to each wire and cross over in a **4mm** bead.

9. Add 1 **3x6** pearl to each wire and cross over to connect band in first **4mm** bead at position **J** shown in **Figure 29.** *Make note of the pattern shown on in Figure 29. The horizontal circumference wrap begins and ends with a 4 bead cross over connected by two 3x6 beads. This pattern may be repeated on the back side of the ornament with special attention to the development of the wrap.*

Vertical wrap

1. Starting at position **J**, run the upper wire through the first top length-wise bead right to left.

2. Run the bottom wire through the first lower lengthwise bead from right to left and up through the second cross over then through the top length-wise bead from left to right.

3. The wires are in place to weave the pattern from position **J** to **K.**

4. Add 1 **3x6** pearl to each wire and cross over in a **4mm** pearl.

5. Repeat stop 4 until you can end the pattern using 4mm pearl **K** to cross over completing the connection.

6. Match your collar to the number of beads shown in Figure 31. If you only have 6 beads at the top of the collar, back weave the wires and trim.

7. If your collar has more than 6 beads, use the wires from K shown above to weave the matching 4mm or 3x6 beads across the col-

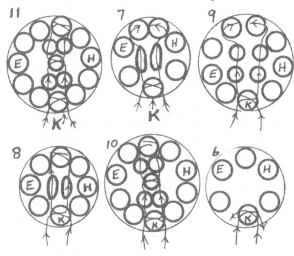

FIGURE 31 Beads woven atop and in the center of the collar on wires from the top K crossover.

lar connecting through the beads shown.

8. Back weave wires to secure and trim.

Cross

Base

1. Using wires from pearl H weave one wire from pearl H around to pearl E. follow the matching diagram shown above in **Figure 32** to weave **4mm** or **3x6** beads over collar from **H** to **E** as shown.

2. Back weave wires to center as shown on diagram. Wires will have one or two beads between them as shown on you **Figure 32.**

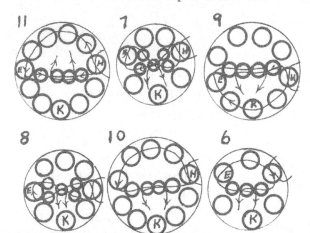

FIGURE 32   Cross base woven on wires from the collar top H crossover.

3. Add 1 4mm pearl to each wire crossing over with a 4mm pearl.

4. Repeat until there are 11 center **4mm** pearls.

5. Secure top wires and twist to create hanger.

Crossbar

1. Center a 4mm pearl on a 7 inch piece of 28 gauge wire.

2. Add 1 4mm pearl to each wire and cross over in 1 4mm pearl.

3. Repeat step 2 once.

4. Add 1 4mm pearl to each wire and feed top wire through 4th center 4mm pearl and bottom wire through 5th center 4mm pearl.

5. Add 1 4mm pearl to each wire and cross over in 1 4mm pearl.

6. Repeat two times. Back weave to secure and trim wires.

Difficulty: Intermediate

Finished size: 3 - 4 inches

Beads:

72 - 5mm gold beads

117 - 4mm gold

9 - 4mm pearl

27 - 3mm pearl

Wire:

1 26 - inch 28 gauge gold

1 36 - inch 28 gauge gold

Chrismons

(CHRISt + MONogramS)

9 Point Crown

The Crown is a symbol for the Kingship of our Lord, Jesus Christ,

the King of kings and Lord of lords.

1 Timothy 6:15

Ascension Lutheran Church
Danville, VA

Lower Band

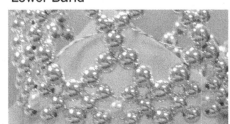

1. Center one **4mm** gold bead on **26 inch** gold wire.
2. Add a **5mm** gold to each wire and CC with one **4mm** gold bead.
3. Add a **4mm** gold to each wire and CC with one **4mm** pearl.
   *
4. Add a **4mm** gold to each wire and CC with one **4mm** gold.
5. Repeat the pattern until you have 9 pearl center beads or 27 total center beads. * Your final center bead should be pearl.
6. Add a **4mm** gold bead to each wire and CC wires in the first gold bead.
7. Run the wires through the next two outside beads and CC in the next center bead to secure the wires.

Crown Points

1. Center a **5mm** gold bead on the **36-inch** gold wire.
2. Add two **5mm** gold beads to wire on one side and three **4mm** beads to wire on other

side.

3. Using the wire with two 5mm beads; run the wire into a 5mm on the lower band. Add two **5mm** gold beads.
4. Using the wire with three 4mm beads add one **5mm** gold bead and three **3mm** pearl beads, weave the wire back into the **5mm** bead (the one

touching the pearl bead), gently tighten the wire and add three **4mm** gold.

5. Using the two wires CC in one gold **5mm** bead.
6. Repeat until you have 9 points.
7. Final CC will connect to first **5mm** gold bead. Weave wires to secure.

Ascension Lutheran Church 314 West Main Street
Danville, Virginia 24540 Phone: 434-792-5795
Web: chrismon.org, Facebook, Pinterest, Etsy
E-mail: chrismonsministry@gmail.com
Copyright 2016 Lutheran Church of the Ascension, Danville, VA

Difficulty: Advanced

Church Size 5" tall

Beads:
29 - 4mm gold
235 - 6mm gold
25 - 14mm gold

Wire:
24 gauge gold
26 gauge gold
28 gauge gold

Home Size 2.5" tall

Beads:
4 - 2mm gold
201 - 3mm gold
25 - 6mm gold

Wire:
24 gauge gold
28 gauge gold

Chrismons

(CHRISt + MONogramS)

The Kingship of our Lord; His Victory over sin and death; His Place of honor at the right hand of the Father.

Chrismons explanation booklet, page 54

Ascension Lutheran Church
Danville, VA

Church Size Crown
Brow Band of the Crown (row1)

96 - 6mm gold
24 - 4mm gold
3 - 24" wire, 26 gauge

1. Center a **6mm** gold on a 24" wire.
2. Put a **6mm** gold on each wire and cross connect (cc) a **6mm** gold.
3. CC a **6mm** gold
4. CC a **4mm** gold
5. Repeat steps 2, 3 & 4 seven (7) more times.
6. Center the last 6mm gold on another 24" wire.

STARTING BROW BAND

7. Put a **6mm** gold on both wires on each side as one wire.
8. CC a **6mm** gold using both Trim shorter wires.
9. CC a **4mm** gold
10. Repeat steps 2, 3 & 4 seven (7) more times
11. Repeat step 6.
12. Repeat steps 7-10 seven (7) more times
13. Close the band by CC thru the 1st **6mm** gold, thread wires thru outside **6mm** gold and CC thru the **6mm** gold. Trim Wires.

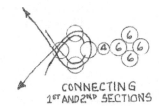
CONNECTING
1ST AND 2ND SECTIONS

Brow Band (row 2)
24 - **14mm** gold   1 - 30" wire, 24 gauge
96 - **6mm** gold   1 - 26" wire, 26 gauge
A variation: Use a 14mm pearl in every 3rd position.

1. Thread all **14mm** gold on the doubled 30" wire and thread one end thru 2 or 3 - 14mm to complete a circle, leaving some space between all beads. Do not trim 24 gauge wire.
2. Secure one end of the 26 gauge wire to the 1st row.

SECURING 26 GA. WIRE

3. Put 5 - **6mm** gold on the 26 gauge wire, over the **14mm** gold.
4. Thread wire thru next upper **6mm** on 1st row and back up thru last **6mm** gold, ensure the 26 gauge wires are on opposite sides of the 24 gauge wire.
5. Put 4 - **3mm** gold, over the **14mm** gold on the 24 gauge wire.
6. Thread wire thru next upper **6mm** gold, back up thru last **6mm** gold.
7. Repeat steps 5 and 6 seven (7) more times. Secure the end of the wire as in diagram.
8. Anchor 2nd 26 gauge wire as in step 2.
9. Thread the end of the new wire up thru the last **6mm**.

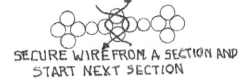

SECURE WIRE FROM A SECTION AND
START NEXT SECTION

10. Repeat steps 5 & 6 eight (8) more times.
11. Anchor 3rd wire and repeat steps 5 & 6 eight (8) more times.
12. Put 3 - **6mm** gold on 26 gauge wire, thread down thru 1st **6mm** gold, thru upper 6mm gold. Secure as in diagram. Trim all wires.

Crown Points (make 8)
1 - **14mm** gold 1 - 12" wire, 26 gauge
35 - **6mm** gold 1 - 10" wire, 26 gauge
5 - **4mm** gold
A variation: Use 6mm pearl in each point.

1. Center a **6mm** gold on the 12" 26 gauge wire and twist wires together below bead.
2. Put both wires as one thru a **14mm** gold and separate wires.
3. Put 4 - **6mm** gold on one wire, wrap around and down thru **14mm** gold.
4. Repeat step 3 on other wire. Tighten both wires snugly.

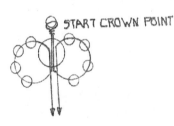

START CROWN POINT

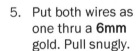

5. Put both wires as one thru a **6mm** gold. Pull snugly.
6. Separate wires and put a **4mm** and a 6mm on each wire.
7. CC thru a **4mm** gold.
8. Find the center of the 10" 26 gauge wire and

STEPS 5, 6 AND 7

STEP 8

form a **6mm** flat like a staple.
9. Thread the wires down thru the side **6mm** gold in step 6 on each side.
10. Put 6 - **6mm** gold on the outside wire on the

---

outside wire on one side and 5 - 6mm gold on the inside wire on same side.

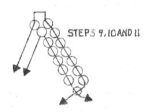

STEPS 9, 10 AND 11

11. CC a **4mm** gold.
12. Repeat steps 10 and 11 on the other side.
13. Continue all of the above steps seven (7) more times.

Connecting Crown Points

8 - **6mm** gold
1. CC a **6mm** on one 26 gauge wire from two points.
2. Thread wire thru the **4mm** on one point.
3. Repeat step 2 on other side of the **4mm**.
4. Pull the two wires snug to join points
5. Wrap each of the wires twice between the **4mm** and **6mm** on the inside of each point, not the 6mm in step 1. Wrap each wire twice between the two lower outside **6mm**. Trim wires.
   Note: Leave the other two wires at the junction to fasten points to brow band.
6. Continue above steps until all eight points are connected.

Attaching Points to Band

1. Thread wires down thru **6mm** as shown in the diagram.
2. Wrap wire twice around 24 gauge wire as shown in the diagram. Trim wires
3. Continue above steps at every third location until all points are connected

Hanger
2 - 10" wire, 28 gauge
1. Find the center of both wires and together, around a pencil or other round object, twist all wires   together about 1/4".
2. Attach the 4 ends to the bow band at equal distances around the brow band.

Home Size Crown
Brow Band of the Crown (row1)

96 - **3mm** gold
2 - 18" wire, 28 gauge

1. Center a **3mm** gold on a 18" wire.
2. Put a **3mm** gold on each wire and cross connect (cc) a **3mm** gold.
3. CC a **3mm** gold

STARTING BROW BAND

4. Repeat steps 2 & 3 eleven (11) more times.
5. Center the last **3mm** gold on the other 18" wire.
6. Put a **3mm** gold on both wires on each side as one wire.
7. CC a **3mm** gold using both wires as one.
8. Trim shorter wires.
9. Repeat steps 2 & 3 eleven (11) more times
10. Close the band by CC thru the 1st **3mm** gold, thread wires thru outside 3mm gold and CC thru the **3mm** gold. Trim wires.

CONNECTING
1ST AND 2ND SECTIONS

Brow Band (row 2)

24 - 6mm gold 1 - 12" wire, 24 gauge
72 - 3mm gold 2 - 18" wire, 28 gauge
A variation: Use a 6mm pearl in every 3rd position.

1. Thread all **6mm** gold on the 12" wire and thread one end thru 2 or 3 - **6mm** to complete a circle, leaving some space between all beads. Do not trim 24 gauge wire.
2. Secure one end of the 28 gauge wire to the 1st row.
3. Put 4– **3mm** gold on the 28 gauge wire, over the **6mm** gold 24 gauge wire.
4. Thread wire thru next upper **3mm** on 1st row and

Securing 28 Gauge Wire

back up thru last **3mm** gold, ensure the 28 gauge wires are on opposite sides of the 24 gauge wire.
5. Put 3 - **4mm** gold, over the 6mm gold on the 24 gauge wire.

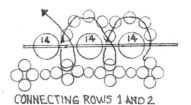

CONNECTING ROWS 1 AND 2.

6. Thread wire thru next upper **3mm** gold.
7. Repeat steps 4 and 5 ten (10) more times. Secure the end of the wire as in diagram.
8. Anchor 2nd 28 gauge wire as in step 2.
9. Thread end of the new wire up thru the last

Securing wire at end.

3mm.

10. Repeat steps 5 & 6 eleven (11) more times.
11. Put 2 - **3mm** gold on 28 gauge wire, thread down thru 1st **3mm** gold, thru upper **3mm** gold. Secure as in step 7. Trim all wires.

Crown Points (make 8)

1 - **6mm** gold   4 - **2mm** gold
33 - **3mm** gold 3 - 12" wire, 28 gauge
A variation: Use 6mm pearl in each point.

1. Center a **3mm** gold on a 28 gauge wire and twist wires to-gether below bead.
2. Put both wires as one thru a **6mm** gold and separate wires.
3. Put 4 - **3mm** gold on one wire, wrap around and down thru **6mm** gold.
4. Repeat step 3 on another wire. Tighten both wires snugly.
5. Put both wires as one thru a **3mm** gold. Pull snugly.
6. Separate wires and put a **2mm** and a **3mm** on

START CROWN POINT

each wire.

7. CC thru a **3mm** gold.
8. Find the center of the remaining 28 gauge wire and form a **3mm** flat like a staple.

STEPS 5, 6 AND 7

STEP 8

9. Thread the wires down thru the side **3mm** gold in step 6 on each side.
10. Put 5 - **3mm** gold on the outside wire on one side and 4 - **3mm** gold on the inside wire on the same side.
11. CC a **2mm** gold.
12. Repeat steps 10 and 11 on the other side.
13. Continue all of the above steps seven (7) more times.

Connecting Crown Points

8 - **3mm** gold

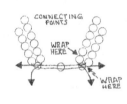

1. CC a **3mm** on one 28 gauge wire from two points.
2. Thread wire thru the **2mm** on one point.
3. Repeat step 2 on other side of the **4mm**.
4. Pull the two wires snug to join points
5. Wrap the wire twice between the **2mm** and **3mm** on the inside of each point, not the **3mm** in step 1. Trim wires. Note: Leave the other two wires at the junction to fasten points to brow band.
6. Continue above steps until all eight points are connected.

Attaching Points to Band

1. Thread wires down thru **3mm** as shown in diagram.
2. Wrap wire twice around 24 gauge wire as shown in diagram.
3. Trim wires
4. Continue above steps at every third location until all points are connected

Hanger

2 - 6" wire, 28 gauge
1. Find the center of both wires and together, around a pencil or other round object, twist all wires together about 1/4".
2. Attach the 4 ends to the bow band at equal distances around the brow band.

For large home-size Crown or a small church-size Crown,
substitute the materials listed below and follow the above instructions.

Lower band: 96 - **4mm** Gold
                2 - 24" wire, 26 or 28 gauge.

Upper band: 24 - **8mm** gold
                72 - **4mm** gold
                1 - 15" wire, 24 gauge
                2 - 18" wire, 28 gauge

Points (each): 1 - **8mm** gold
                35 - **4mm** gold*
                4 - **3mm** gold
                1 - 12" wire, 28 gauge
                1 - 10" wire, 28 gauge

Connecting Points: 8 - **4mm** gold

*In the instructions for Grown Points, Step 10: put 6 - 4mm gold on the outside wire and 5 - 4mm gold on the inside wire on the same side.

Chrismons™ Ornaments

Ascension Lutheran Church 314 West Main Street
Danville, Virginia 24540 Phone: 434-792-5795
Web: chrismon.org Facebook, Pinterest, Etsy
E-mail: chrismonsministry@gmail.com
Copyright 2016 Lutheran Church of the Ascension, Danville, VA

Iota Chi Cross

Difficulty: Beginner

Finished size: 2.25 inches

Beads:

6   6mm gold

12 5mm gold

12 4mm gold

Wires:

28-inch 26 gauge gold

Chrismons

(CHRISt + MONogramS)

Iota Chi
IX

The Iota (I) is the first letter of our Lord's given name Jesus in Greek. This name means "the promised one."

The Chi(X) is the first letter of his Greek title Christ. Christos (XPISTOS), is the translation of the Hebrew "Messiah", which means "the one anointed by God."

When these two letters are superimposed, they become our Savior's cipher, the symbolic interweaving of initials that some people call a star.

Ascension Lutheran Church

Danville, Virginia

The Monogram of Christ Jesus.

The Iota Chi has six legs that will be made in sequence.

1. Center one 6mm bead on the wire.
2. Stack two 5mm beads and two 4mm beads on both wires.
3. Pull wires tight.
4. Add two 4mm, two 5mm and one 6mm onto one wire.
5. Return weave the wire through the two 5mm and two 4mm beads.
6. Pull wires tight.

7. Add two 4mm, two 5mm and one 6mm onto the same wire.
8. **Return weave through the two 5mm and two 4mm beads.**
9. Pull wires tight.
10. Add two 4mm, two 5mm and one 6mm onto the second wire.
11. **Return weave through the two 5mm and two 4mm beads.**
12. Pull wires tight.

13. Add two 4mm, two 5mm and one 6mm onto the same wire.
14. **Return weave through the two 5mm and two 4mm beads.**
15. Pull wires tight.

16. Add two 4mm and two 5mm beads to both wires.

17. Cross over with one 6mm bead and twist.
18. Create Hanger.

39

Ascension Lutheran Church 314 West Main Street
Danville, Virginia 24540 Phone: 434-792-5795
Web: chrismon.org Facebook, Pinterest, Etsy
E-mail: chrismonsministry@gmail.com
Copyright 2014 Lutheran Church of the Ascension, Danville, VA

Difficulty: Intermediate

Finished size: 4 inches

Beads:
30 3x6mm pearl
30 5mm pearl
30 6mm pearl
24 3mm gold
29 4mm gold

Wires:
1 45-inch 28 gauge Silver
1 20 - inch 28 gauge gold
1 28 - inch 28 gauge gold

Chrismons

(CHRISt + MONogramS)

Iota Chi in Eternity

*Jesus Christ at the center of
God's everlasting love.*

IX and Circle

The Iota (I) is the first letter of
our Lord's given name Jesus in
Greek. This name means "the
promised one."

The Chi (X) is the first letter of
his Greek title Christos, "the
one anointed by God."

The never ending circle represents God's everlasting love for
us.

Ascension Lutheran Church

Danville, Virginia

Circle

1. Center one **3x6** pearl bead on 45-inch 28-gauge silver wire.

2. Add one **5mm** and one **6mm** pearl bead on each side.

3. CC with one **3x6** pearl bead.

4. Repeat until you have used 30 **3x6** pearls beads, keeping all 5mm beads on the inside and 6mm beads on the outside.

5. Add last **5mm** and **6mm** pearl beads, close circle and create hanger.

IOTA - I

1. Center 20-inch gold wire in top 5mm pearl bead.

2. Add one **3mm** gold bead to each side and CC with one **4mm** gold bead.

3. Add one **3mm** bead to each side and CC with one **4mm** bead.

4. Repeat 9 times. You will have 11 center **4mm** beads.

5. Add one **3mm** to each side.

6. Return weave thru outer circle.

Chi - X

1. Center 26-inch gold wire in the 5th from top (do not count top bead) **5mm** pearl bead.

2. Add 5 **4mm** gold beads to both wires.

3. Separate the wires and add 4 **4mm** beads to wire one.

4. Weave wire one through the 10th from top (do not count top bead) **5mm** pearl bead.

5. Return weave wire one through the previous 4 beads.

6. Crossover in bead number 5 from double wires.

7. Pull wires tight.

8. Weave both wires through center of Iota, starting between the **3mm** beads moving through the **3mm** bead up or down to the **4mm** bead and through **3mm** bead on other side ending between the **3mm** beads.

9. Crossover with one **4mm** gold bead on opposite side.

10. Add 4 **4mm** gold beads to bottom wire.

11. Weave bottom wire through the 5th from bottom (do not count bottom bead) **5mm** pearl bead.

12. Return weave bottom wire through the previous 4 beads.

13. Weave wire through first crossover bead.

14. Add 4 **4mm** beads to both wires.

15. Back weave both wires in 10th from bottom (do not count bottom bead) **5mm** pearl bead.

Chrismons™ Ornaments

Ascension Lutheran Church 314 West Main Street
Danville, Virginia 24540 Phone: 434-792-5795
Web: chrismon.org   Facebook, Pinterest, Etsy
E-mail: chrismonsministry@gmail.com
Copyright 2016 Lutheran Church of the Ascension, Danville, VA

Iota Eta Sigma on a Greek Cross

Difficulty: Intermediate

Finished size: 4.25 inches

Beads:

16   8mm gold

48   6mm gold

20   5mm gold

105 3mm gold

Wires:

2 18-inch 26 gauge gold

3 12-inch 28 gauge silver

1 14-inch 28 gauge silver

Chrismons

(CHRISt + MONogramS)

Greek Cross

With

Iota Eta Sigma

The first three letters of JESUS in Greek

compose this monogram.

i h c

The monogram hangs on a Greek Cross to

remind us of our Savior's sacrifice for all mankind.

Ascension Lutheran Church

Danville, Virginia

Greek Cross

Arm of Cross

1. Fold one gold 26 gauge wire in half.
2. Center three **8mm** gold beads on wire.
3. CC with one **8mm** gold bead.
4. Add one **6mm** gold bead to each wire. CC with one **6mm** gold.
5. Repeat until you have completed 8 CC with **6mm** beads.
6. Add one 6mm gold bead to each wire. CC with one **8mm** gold.
7. Add one **8mm** bead to each wire. CC with one **8mm** gold bead.
8. Back weave wires to secure.

Upright of Cross

1. Fold second gold 26 gauge wire in half.
2. Center three 8mm gold beads on wire.
3. CC with one 8mm Gold Bead.
4. Add one 6mm gold bead to each wire. CC with one 6mm gold.
5. Repeat until you have completed 3 CC with 6mm beads.
6. Add one 6mm gold bead to each wire.
7. Feed wires through the 4th and 5th beads of the previously completed strand.
8. Add one 6mm gold bead to each wire. CC with one 6mm bead.
9. Repeat until you have 3 center 6mm beads on each side of cross.
10. Add one 6mm gold bead to each wire. CC with one 8mm gold.
11. Add one 8mm gold to each wire. CC with one 8mm bead.
12. Twist wires to create a hanger.

Monogram h.

1. Fold one 12-inch silver wire in half.
2. Center three 5mm pearl beads on the wire. CC with one 5mm pearl bead.
3. Add one 3mm pearl to each wire. CC with one 3mm pearl.
4. Repeat until you have six 3mm center beads.
5. Add two 3mm pearl beads to one wire and one 3mm pearl to the other wire.
6. String 7 more 3mm pearl beads onto both wires. Total of 8 .
7. Weave both wires back through the 5th trough the 6th bead.

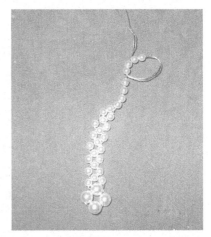

8. Cut both wires.

9. Fold 14-inch wire in half and center on 4th inner 3mm bead from the bottom of h.
10. Add five 3mm pearl beads to both wires.
11. Add two 3mm pearl beads to upper wire.
12. CC with one 3mm pearl bead.
13. Add one 3mm pearl bead to each wire. CC with one 3mm pearl.
14. Repeat until you have eight 3mm center beads.
15. Add two 3mm pearl beads to outside (right) wire and one 3mm pearl to the inner (left) wire.
16. String eight 3mm pearl beads onto both wires.
17. Weave one wire back through the 5th through 6th bead.
18. Cut both wires.

Monogram c.

1. Fold second 12-inch silver wire in half.
2. Center three 5mm peal beads on the wire. CC with one 5mm pearl bead.
3. Add one 3mm pearl bead to each wire.
4. CC with one 3mm pearl bead.
5. Add two 3mm pearl beads to one wire and one 3mm pearl to the other wire.
6. String three 3mm pearl beads onto both wires.
7. Add one 3mm pearl bead to each wire. CC with one 3mm pearl bead.
8. Repeat one time.
9. Add one 3mm peal bead to each wire.
10. String three 3mm pearl beads onto both wires.
11. Add two 3mm pearl beads to top wire and one 3mm pearl to the bottom wire. CC with one 3mm pearl bead.
12. Add one 3mm pearl bead to each wire. CC with one 5mm pearl bead.
13. Add one 5mm pearl bead to each wire. CC with one 5mm pearl bead.
14. Back weave to secure.

Monogram i.

1. Fold third 12-inch silver wire in half.
2. Center three 5mm pearl beads on the wire. CC with one 5mm pearl bead.
3. Add one 3mm pearl bead to each wire. CC with one 3mm pearl bead.
4. Repeat until you have four 3mm center beads.
5. Add one 3mm pearl bead to each wire. CC with one 5mm pearl bead.
6. Add one 5mm pearl bead to each wire. CC with one 5mm pearl bead.
7. Back weave to secure.
8. Attach ihc to the cross.

Note : The Sigma "S"symbol may also be used. Reference Figure 17 page 35 Chrismons Basic Series.

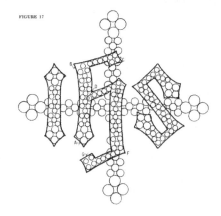

FIGURE 17

Iota Eta Sigma in Eternity version

Complete cross as described on previous page.

36 **8mm** gold beads
1 12-inch 26 gauge gold wire

1. Feed 12" wire through one end 8mm gold bead on a cross arm and center wire.
2. String 9 **8mm** gold beads on wire. Feed end of wire through the next cross arm at the end **8mm** bead. Repeat step 2 secure the wire by back weaving.
3. With other half of the 12" wire working in the opposite direction, repeat step 2 twice completing the eternity circle.
4. Secure wires.

Chrismons™ Ornaments

Ascension Lutheran Church 314 West Main Street
Danville, Virginia 24540 Phone: 434-792-5795
Web: chrismon.org Facebook, Pinterest, Etsy
E-mail: chrismonsministry@gmail.com
Copyright 2016 Lutheran Church of the Ascension, Danville, VA

Jesus Cross

Difficulty: Intermediate

Finished size: 3.5 inches

Beads:

132 5x7mm pearls

16 8mm pearls

Wires:

4   16-inch 28 gauge silver

4   20-inch 28 gauge silver

Chrismons

(CHRISt + MONogramS)

Jesus Cross

The Cross is always a reminder of our Lord's saving work of redeeming mankind through His sacrifice for our sins, by which we receive forgiveness and salvation.

The Latin Cross is the most widely used form of the cross today.

The Cross of Jesus is filled with God's Eternal Love.

The Last Supper

Ascension Lutheran Church
Danville, VA

Upright of Cross

1. Fold first 20-inch wire in half.
2. Place three 5x7mm beads on first wire.
3. Crossover with one 5x7mm bead
4. Repeat with second 20-inch wire.
5. Fold third 20-inch wire in half .
6. Place one 5x7mm beads on third wire.
7. Thread one side of third wire into one side bead of the first wire.
8. Thread other side of third wire into one side bead of the second wire.
9. Crossover with one 5x7mm bead.
10. Fold fourth 20-inch wire in half .
11. Place one 5x7mm bead on fourth wire.
12. Thread one side of fourth wire into the remaining side bead of the first wire and the other side of the fourth wire into the remaining side bead of the second wire.
13. Crossover with one 5x7mm bead.
14. Insert one 8mm bead into the box and pull all wires tight.
15. At this point you will have eight wires above 3 rows of 4 concentric beads.
16. Add four beads, one to each corner of double wires.
17. Crossover four beads using one wire from each corner.
18. Insert one 8mm bead into the box and pull all wires tight.
19. Repeat until you have 10 boxes with 10 beads inside.
20. To end, return weave one wire from each corner. Use remaining four wires to create a hanger.

Arms of Cross

1. Fold first 16-inch wire in half.
2. Place three 5x7mm beads on first wire.
3. Crossover with one 5x7mm bead.
4. Repeat with second 16-inch wire.
5. Fold third 16-inch wire in half .
6. Place one 5x7mm beads on third wire.
7. Thread one side of third wire into one side bead of the first wire.
8. Thread other side of third wire into one side bead of the second wire.
9. Crossover with one 5x7mm bead.

10. Fold fourth 16-inch wire in half .
11. Place one 5x7mm bead on fourth wire.
12. Thread one side of fourth wire into the remaining side bead of the first wire and the other side of the fourth wire into the remaining side bead of the second wire.
13. Crossover with one 5x7mm bead.
14. Insert one 8mm bead into box, pull all wires tight.
15. At this point you will have eight wires above one box.
16. Add four beads, one to each corner of double wires.
17. Crossover four beads using one wire from each corner.
18. Insert one 8mm bead into box, pull all wires tight.
19. Repeat for second box.
20. Add four beads, one to each corner of double wires.
21. Weave double corner wires through 4th and 5th 5x7 beads on each side of the upright.
22. Insert an 8mm bead and pull cross arm tight to upright.
23. Add four beads, one to each corner of double wires.
24. Crossover four beads using one wire from each corner.
25. Insert one 8mm bead into box, pull all wires tight.
26. Repeat until you have 3 boxes on this side of the upright.
27. To end, return weave all wires.

Chrismons™ Ornaments

Ascension Lutheran Church 314 West Main Street
Danville, Virginia 24540 Phone: 434-792-5795
Web: chrismon.org Facebook, Pinterest, Etsy
E-mail: chrismonsministry@gmail.com
Copyright 2014 Lutheran Church of the Ascension, Danville, VA

Latin Cross

Difficulty: Beginner

Finished size: 5 inches

Beads:

34   8mm gold

26   10mm gold

Wires:

18 - inch 24 gauge gold

24 - inch 28 gauge gold

Chrismons
(CHRISt + MONogramS)

Latin Cross

The Cross is always a reminder of our Lord's saving work of redeeming mankind through His sacrifice for our sins, by which we receive forgiveness and salvation.

The Latin Cross is the most widely used form of the cross today.

Ascension Lutheran Church
Danville, VA

Upright of Cross:

1. Center one 10mm bead on the 24 inch, 28- gauge wire.
2. Add one 10mm bead to one wire and return weave.
3. Add one 10mm bead to other wire and return weave.
4. Check that the wires are the same length.
5. You should see "Mouse Ears".
6. Turn mouse ears over and add one 8mm bead to each wire.
7. Crossover with one 10mm bead. Pull wires tight.
8. Add one 8mm bead to each wire.
9. Cross over with one 10mm bead.
10. Repeat 8 times.

11. There should be a total of eleven 10mm beads in the center of the upright of the cross.
12. Add one 10mm bead to one wire and return weave in the center 10mm bead. Pull tight.
13. Add one 10mm bead to other wire and return weave in same center 10mm bead. Pull tight.
14. Twist wires to make a hanger.

Crossbar:

1. Center one 8mm bead on the 18 inch, 24-gauge wire.
2. Add one 10 mm bead on one wire and return weave.
3. Add one 10mm bead to other wire and return weave.

4. Check that the wires are the same length.
5. You should see "Mouse Ears".
6. Add one 8mm bead to each wire.
7. Crossover with one 10mm bead. Pull wires tight.
8. Repeat until there are three 10mm center beads in the arm of the cross.
9. Add one 8mm bead to each wire.
10. Thread the two wires through the 4th and 5th 10mm bead from the top of the upright.
11. Pull wires tight.
12. Add one 8mm bead to each wire.
13. Crossover with one 10mm bead.
14. Repeat twice and you should have three 10mm center beads on the arm.
15. Add one 10mm bead to one wire and return weave in the center 10mm bead. Pull tight.
16. Add one 10mm bead to other wire and return weave in same center 10mm bead. Pull tight.
17. Secure wires by running each wire back through the previous 8mm bead.
18. Cross over in the closest 10mm bead. Pull wires tight and cut.

Chrismons™ Ornaments

Ascension Lutheran Church 314 West Main Street
Danville, Virginia 24540 Phone: 434-792-5795
Web: chrismon.org Facebook, Pinterest, Etsy
E-mail: chrismonsministry@gmail.com
Copyright 2016 Lutheran Church of the Ascension, Danville, VA

Latin Cross with Alpha and Omega

Difficulty: Beginner

Finished size: 5 inches

Beads:

42 6mm gold

30 8mm gold

6 4mm pearl

24 3mm pearl

Wires:

18 - inch 26 gauge gold

26 - inch 28 gauge gold

4 6 - inch 28 gauge silver

Chrismons
(CHRISt + MONogramS)

Latin Cross

With Hanging

Alpha & Omega

The Cross is always a reminder of our Lord's saving work of redeeming mankind through His sacrifice for our sins, by which we receive forgiveness and salvation

The Hanging Alpha and Omega remind us

"I am Alpha and the Omega, the first and the last, the beginning and the end". Revelations 22:13; Isaiah 44:6; Isaiah 48:12.

Ascension Lutheran Church
Danville, Virginia

Upright of Cross

1. Center one **8mm** gold on the 26-inch 28 gauge wire.
2. Add one **8mm** bead to each side and return weave.
3. Add one **6mm** bead to each wire and crossover with one 8mm bead.

4. Repeat 12 times. *There should be a total of 14 8mm beads in the center of the upright of the cross.*
5. Add one 8mm bead to each wire, return weave in center **8mm** bead.
6. Twist wires to make hanger.

Arms of Cross

1. Center one 8mm bead on the 18-inch 26 gauge wire.
2. Add one **8mm** bead to each side and return weave.
3. Add one **6mm** bead to each wire and crossover with one **8mm** bead.
4. Repeat 2 times.
5. Add one 6mm bead to each wire. *There should be a total of four 8mm beads in the center of the arm of the cross and 1 loose 6mm bead on each wire.*

6. Thread the two wires through the 5th and 6th **8mm** bead from the top of the upright.
7. Add one **6mm** bead to each wire and crossover with one **8mm** bead.
8. Repeat 3 times.
9. Add one **8mm** bead to each wire, return weave in center **8mm** bead.
10. Secure wires by running each wire back through the previous 6mm bead and crossover in the closest **8mm** bead.

Alpha and Omega

See page 43 for Figure 3 diagram from the Chrismons Basic Book page 20.

Alpha

1. Fold one 6" piece of 28 gauge wire and center 1 **4mm** bead.

2. Hold the wire ends slightly apart between the thumb and forefinger about one-half inch from the bead; turn the bead so that the wires twist on themselves next to the bead.

3. String two **3mm** pearl beads on both wires.

4. Repeat steps 1 - 3 with second wire.

5. Place two **3mm** pearls on long wire of one leg.

6. Take the long wire of the second leg and feed it

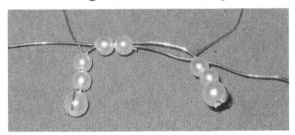

through the same two **3mm** pearls in step 5.

7. Pull the crossed over wires tight and bend them upward.

8. String two **3mm** pearls over both wires at each side.

9. Feed both long wires through one 4mm bead at the top use remaining long wires to attach to the Cross. You may want to loop one wire to secure if not attaching yet.

10. Trim short wires.

Omega

1. Fold one 6 inch piece of 28 gauge wire and center a **4mm** bead.

2. Hold the wire ends slightly apart between the thumb and forefinger about one-half inch from the bead; turn the bead so that the wires twist on themselves next to the bead.

3. String 7 **3mm** pearl beads on both wires.

4. Repeat with second wire to create other leg of Omega.

5. Cross over the long wire of each leg through a **4mm** pearl and pull tight.

6. Return weave to secure and use long wires to secure to the cross.

Steps 1-3   Step 5

Letters can be attached through a bead or between two beads to be more securely attached.

Chrismons™ Ornaments

Flared Latin Cross

Ascension Lutheran Church 314 West Main Street
Danville, Virginia 24540 Phone: 434-792-5795
Web: chrismon.org, Facebook, Pinterest, Etsy
E-mail: chrismonsministry@gmail.com
Copyright 2016 Lutheran Church of the Ascension, Danville, VA

Difficulty: Intermediate

Finished size: 2.5 inches

Beads:

12 3mm gold

54 4mm gold

41 5mm gold

Wires:

22 - inch 28 gauge gold

15 - inch 28 gauge gold

Chrismons

(CHRISt + MONogramS)

Flared Latin Cross

The Cross is always a reminder of our Lord's saving work of redeeming mankind through His sacrifice for our sins, by which we receive forgiveness and salvation.

The Latin Cross is the most widely used form of the cross today.

Ascension Lutheran Church
Danville, Virginia

Upright of Cross

1. Center one 5mm gold bead on the 14-inch 28 gauge wire.
2. Add one 4mm gold bead to each side and
3. crossover with one 5mm gold bead.
4. Add one 3mm, two 5mm, one 3mm, one 4mm and one 3mm to each wire.
5. Turn upright over.
6. Crossover in first 5mm bead.
7. Add one 4mm bead to each side and
8. crossover with one 5mm pearl bead.
9. Repeat 12 times
10. Add one 3mm, two 5mm, one 3mm, one 4mm and one 3mm to each wire.
11. Crossover in second 5mm bead from bottom of upright.
12. Run wires down through 4mm beads a second time
13. Crossover in 5mm bead a second time.
14. Twist wires to make a hanger.

Crossbar of Cross

1. Center one 5mm gold bead on the 14-inch 28 gauge wire.
2. Add one 4mm gold bead to each side and
3. crossover with one 5mm gold bead.
4. Add one 3mm, two 5mm, one 3mm, one 4mm and one 3mm

to each wire.
5. Turn upright over.
6. Crossover in first 5mm bead.
7. Add one 4mm bead to each side and
8. crossover with one 5mm pearl bead.
9. Repeat 2 times.
10. Add one 4mm bead to each side.
11. Thread the two wires through the 5th and 6th
12. 5mm bead from the top of the upright.
13. Add one 4mm bead to each side
14. crossover with one 5mm bead.
15. Repeat 3 times.
16. Add one 3mm, two 5mm, one 3mm, 4mm and one 3mm to each wire.
17. Crossover in second 5mm bead from end of crossbar.
18. Moving toward the center of the cross un wires through 4mm beads a second time
19. Crossover in next 5mm bead a second time.
20. Cut wires.

47

Chrismons™ Ornaments

Ascension Lutheran Church 314 West Main Street
Danville, Virginia 24540 Phone: 434-792-5795
Web: chrismon.org Facebook, Pinterest, Etsy
E-mail: chrismonsministry@gmail.com
Copyright 2014 Lutheran Church of the Ascension, Danville, VA

Latin with Trefoil

Difficulty: Beginner

Finished size: 2.5 inches

Beads:

37 5mm gold

12 6mm pearl

Wires:

12 - inch 28 gauge gold

14 - inch 28 gauge gold

Chrismons

(CHRISt + MONogramS)

Latin Cross

With Trefoil

The Cross is always a reminder of our Lord's sacrifice for our sins, by which we receive forgiveness and salvation.

The white Trefoil represents the Holy Trinity, always with us.

Ascension Lutheran Church
Danville, Virginia

Upright of Cross

1. Center three 6mm pearl beads on the 14-inch 28 gauge wire.
2. Crossover with one 5mm gold bead.
3. Add one 5mm gold bead to each wire.
4. Crossover with one 5mm gold bead.
5. Repeat until you have 9 gold center beads.
6. Add one 6mm pearl bead to each wire.
7. Crossover with one 6mm pearl bead.
8. Twist the two wires to create a hanger.

Arms of Cross

1. Center three 6mm pearl beads on the 12-inch 28 gauge wire.
2. Crossover with one 5mm gold bead.
3. Add one 5mm gold bead to each wire.
4. Crossover with one 5mm gold bead.
5. Add one 5mm gold bead to each wire.
6. Thread the two wires through the 3rd and 4th center gold bead from the top of the upright.
7. Add one 5mm gold bead to each wire.
8. Crossover with one 5mm bead.
9. Repeat once.
10. Add one 6mm pearl bead to each wire.
11. Crossover with one 6mm pearl bead.
12. Back weave until secure.
13. Cut wires.

Chrismons™ Ornaments

Ascension Lutheran Church 314 West Main Street
Danville, Virginia 24540 Phone: 434-792-5795
Web: chrismon.org Facebook, Pinterest, Etsy
E-mail: chrismonsministry@gmail.com
Copyright 2016 Lutheran Church of the Ascension, Danville, VA

Paired Latin Crosses Fusilee - Small

Difficulty: Advanced

Finished size: 4.5 inches

Beads:

Cross - gold (makes 2)
44 6mm   108 4mm

Alpha - pearl beads
74 4mm   46 5mm

Omega - peal beads
10 3mm   72 4mm
44 5mm

Wire:

28 gauge silver & gold

26 gauge gold

Passion Cross
with
Alpha and Omega

The paired Latin Crosses Fusilee,
one entwined with an Alpha
another with an Omega
remind us

"I am Alpha and the Omega,
the first and the last,
the beginning and the end".
Revelations 22:13; Isaiah 44:6; Isaiah 48:12.

The pointed ends of the
Cross Fusilee, also known as the
Passion Cross
(or Cross of Suffering), remind us
of the points of the thorns, the
nails, and the spear.
John 19.

*Ascension Lutheran Church
Danville, Virginia*

Small Passion Cross

22 6mm Gold beads
108 4mm Gold beads

14-inch 26 gauge gold wire
20-inch 28 gauge gold wire

Upright of Cross

1. String 3 **4mm** beads and loosely crossover 1 **6mm** bead in the center of the 28 gauge wire.

2. Gently turn center **4mm** bead one full twist to create a pointed end to the cross.

3. Add 1 **4mm** bead to each wire and crossover with 1 **6mm** bead.

4. Repeat 12 times.

5. *There should be a total of 14 6mm beads on the upright of the cross.*

6. Add 1 **4mm** bead to each wire.

7. Thread both wires straight up into 1 more **4mm** bead.

8. Take one wire under the **4mm** bead and thread through the bead again and tighten.

9. Twist the two wires to create a hanger.

Arms of Cross

1. String 3 **4mm** beads and loosely crossover 1 **6mm** bead in the center of the 26 gauge wire.

2. Gently turn center **4mm** bead one full twist to create a pointed end.

3. Add 1 **4mm** bead to each wire and crossover with 1 **6mm** bead.

4. Repeat 2 times.

5. *There should be a total of 4 6mm beads on each arm of the cross.*

6. Add 1 **4mm** bead to each wire.

7. Thread the two wires through the 5th and 6th large bead from the top of the upright.

8. Add 1 **4mm** bead to each wire and crossover with 1 **6mm** bead.

9. Repeat 3 times.

10. Add 3 **4mm** bead to one wire.

11. Gently twist center bead

12. Thread wire through opposite side of **6mm** bead

13. Back weave until secure.

Small Alpha

74 **4mm** Pearl beads

46 **5mm** Pearl beads

2 20-inch 28 gauge silver wire

1 12-inch 28 gauge silver wire

49

1. Center 1 **5mm** bead on 1 20-inch 28 gauge wire.
2. Add 1 **5mm** bead to each side and return weave.
3. Add 1 **4mm** bead to each wire and crossover with 1 **5mm** bead.
4. *Repeat 12 times. **There should be a total of 14 5mm beads on the upright of the cross.***
5. Repeat these instructions on second 20-inch 28 gauge wire.

Joining Legs of Alpha

1. Using 2 woven legs of the A
2. Thread 1 wire from each leg straight up into 1 **4mm** bead.
3. Add 1 **4mm** bead to second wire of each leg.
4. Crossover with 1 **5mm** beads on each side of the center bead.
5. Thread 1 wire from each leg straight up into 1 **5mm** bead
6. Add 1 **4mm** bead to each second wire.
7. Crossover with 1 **4mm** beads on each side of the center bead.
8. Thread 1 wire from each leg straight up into 1 **5mm** bead
9. Crossover with 1 **5mm** bead on each side.
10. Back weave to each wire through 1 bead.
11. Collect all wires on one side of the A and cut 2 leaving 2 wires.

Adding Cross Bar to Alpha

1. Thread 12-inch wire through 6th inside small bead from the bottom of one leg of the A.
2. Add 1 **4mm** bead to each wire and cross over with **5mm** bead.
3. Repeat 1 times.
4. Add 1 **4mm** bead to the top wire.
5. Add 1 **5mm** bead to the bottom wire.
6. Loosely crossover with 1 **5mm** bead (this is the end bead).
7. Backward weave upper wire through 1 **4mm** bead and 1 **5mm** bead.
8. Add 1 **4mm**, 1 **5mm** and 1 **4mm** bead to the same wire.
9. Take the wire up through the end bead (**5mm**)

one more time.
10. Gently pull all wires tight.
11. Add 1 **4mm** bead to each side.
12. Crossover with 1 **5mm** bead.
13. Add 1 **4mm** bead to each wire.
14. Connect to opposite leg of cross at the 6th small inside bead from the bottom. Crossover the wires in the **4mm** bead, take the wires through the closest large beads and crossover on the outside small bead.
15. Trim the wires.

Small Omega

10 **3mm** Pearl beads

72 **4mm** Pearl beads

44 **5mm** Pearl beads

45-inch 28 gauge silver wire

1. Center 1 **5mm** bead on 1 long 28 gauge wire.
2. Add 1 **5mm** bead to each side and return weave.
3. Add 1 **4mm** bead to each wire and crossover with 1 **5mm** bead.
4. Add 2 **4mm** beads to the inside wire and crossover with 1 **5mm** bead.
5. Add 2 4mm beads to the inside wire and 1 **4mm** bead to the outside wire.
6. Crossover with 1 **5mm** bead.
7. Add 1 **4mm** bead to each wire and crossover with 1 **5mm** bead.
8. Repeat 31 times.
9. Add 2 **4mm** beads to the inside wire and 1 4mm bead to the outside wire.
10. Crossover with 1 **5mm** bead.
11. Add 2 **4mm** beads to the inside wire and crossover with 1 **5mm** bead.
12. Add 1 **4mm** bead to each wire and crossover with 1 **5mm** bead.
13. Repeat 1 time.
14. Add 1 **5mm** bead to each side and return weave.

Chrismons™ Ornaments

Ascension Lutheran Church 314 West Main Street
Danville, Virginia 24540 Phone: 434-792-5795
Web: chrismon.org Facebook, Pinterest, Etsy
E-mail: chrismonsministry@gmail.com
Copyright 2016 Lutheran Church of the Ascension, Danville, VA

Maltese Cross

Difficulty: Intermediate

Finished size: 2.25 inches

Beads:

40 3mm gold

4 5mm gold

40 4mm gold

5 5mm Pearl

Wire

4 12-inch 28 gauge gold

Chrismons

(CHRISt + MONogramS)

The Maltese Cross
St. John's Cross

Four Arms of the Cross
Four Cardinal Virtues
Prudence Temperance
Justice Fortitude

The eight points stand for
The Beatitudes *Matthew 5:1-11*
or
The Obligations of a Knight
Live in truth. Have faith.
Be sincere. Give proof of humility.
Love justice. Be merciful.
Endure persecution.
Repent of sin.

Ascension Lutheran Church
Danville, Virginia

Create four tips.

1. Center one 3mm gold bead.
2. Add one 3mm gold to each wire.
3. Crossover with one 3mm gold.
4. Add one 4mm gold bead to each wire,
5. Crossover with one 4mm gold.
6. Repeat with all wires. *You now have four tips each with four 3mm gold beads and three 4mm gold beads.*

7. Using two tips, Take one wire from each tip and crossover in one 3mm gold bead.
8. Add one 4mm gold to the other wire of each tip.
9. Using two wires from each tip, crossover in one 5mm gold bead.
10. Add one 4mm gold bead to both wires on each side.
11. Crossover using both wires on each side in one 5mm pearl bead.
12. Repeat with remaining two tips. *You now have two legs each with one 5mm gold bead and one 5mm pearl bead.*

Create the crossbar

1. Using one leg
2. Add one 3mm gold bead to both wires on each side.
3. Using one wire from each side crossover in one pearl bead.
4. Using the other leg
5. Add one 3mm gold bead to both wires on each side.

6. Using one wire from each side crossover in the last pearl on the other leg. *You now have a completed crossbar with two 5mm gold beads and three 5mm pearl beads*
.

Create the Upright

1. Using wires on one side of the Crossbar—Crossover in one pearl bead using one wire from the 3mm and one wire from the center pearl crossover, on each side.
2. Add one 4mm gold to both wires on each side
3. Crossover in one 5mm gold bead
4. Using one wire from each side—Crossover in one 3mm gold bead
5. Add one 4mm gold to the remaining wire on each side
6. Using one wire from the 3mm gold and one wire from 4mm gold Crossover in one 4mm gold bead.
7. Repeat on the other side of the Crossbar.

Create tips on Upright.

1. Using four sets of wires—Add one 4mm bead to each side and crossover in one 3mm bead.
2. Add one 3mm bead to each side and crossover in one 3mm bead.
3. Back weave on one side of the upright.
4. Create Hanger on the other.

Chrismons™ Ornaments
Ascension Lutheran Church 314 West Main Street
Danville, Virginia 24540 Phone: 434-792-5795
Web: chrismon.org Facebook, Pinterest, Etsy
E-mail: chrismonsministry@gmail.com
Copyright 2014 Lutheran Church of the Ascension, Danville, VA

Music Crosses

Difficulty: Intermediate

Finished size: 5 inches

Beads & Wire

Cross

222   3mm gold

2 22-inch 28 gauge gold

2 12-inch 28 gauge gold

Treble Clef

144   3mm pearl

1 22-inch 28 gauge silver

1 15-inch 28 gauge silver

Notes

98   3mm pearl

1 15-inch 28 gauge silver

1 11-inch 28 gauge silver

**Sing
&
Make Music
In Your
Heart to the Lord**

Speak to one another with psalms, hymns and spiritual songs. Always giving thanks to God the Father for everything, in the name of our Lord Jesus Christ.

Ephesians 5:19-20

Chrismons
Ascension Lutheran Church

Upright

1. Fold first 18-inch gold wire in half.   Center one gold bead.
2. Add one gold bead to each side.   Crossover with one gold bead.
3. Fold second 18-inch gold wire in half.
4. Thread one wire through one outside bead of first 18-inch.
5. Add two beads to other wire of second 18-inch wire.
6. Crossover with a gold bead using two wires from second 18-inch wire.
7. Add one gold bead to two single outside wires and to double inside wire.
8. Add two crossovers using one inside and one outside wire from each side.
9. Repeat until you have 28 beads in the very center row,
10. ending with a crossover.

```
|   ||   |
O   O   O

|   ||   |
\  /\  /

O    O
/  \/  \

O   O   O
```

Crossbar

1. Fold first 12-inch gold wire in half.
2. Center one gold bead.
3. Add one gold bead to each side.
4. Crossover with one gold bead.
5. Fold second 12-inch gold wire in half.
6. Thread one wire through one outside bead of first 18-inch.
7. Add two bead to other wire of

second 18-inch wire.

8. Crossover with a gold bead using two wires from second 18-inch wires.
9. Add one gold bead to two single outside wires and to double inside wire.
10. Add two crossovers using one inside and one outside wire from each side.
11. Repeat until you have 7 beads in the very center, ending with a crossover.
12. Add one gold bead to two single outside wires and to double inside wire.
13. Insert the top single wire into the 8th set of double beads from the top, insert the center two wires into the 9th set of double beads and insert the bottom single wire into the 10th set of double beads.
14. Add one gold bead to two single outside wires and to double inside wire.
15. Add two crossovers using one inside and one outside wire from each side.
16. Repeat until you have 7 beads

in the very center, ending with a crossover.
17. The two arms of the cross should be identical.
18. Back weave to secure wires.

Treble Clef

1. Fold 22-inch silver wire in half.
2. Center one pearl bead on wire.
3. Hold two wires together and add three pearl beads to both wires.
4. Add one pearl bead to each wire.
5. Crossover with one pearl bead.
6. Repeat eight times. *You now have 4 single beads and 9 crossovers.*
7. Add one pearl bead to each wire.
8. Hold two wires together and add 14 pearl beads to both wires.
9. Add one pearl bead to each wire.
10. Crossover with one pearl bead.
11. Repeat 14 times.
12. Add one pearl bead to each wire.
13. Hold two wires together and add five pearl beads to both wires.
14. Add one pearl bead to one wire
15. and two pearl beads to the other wire.
16. Crossover with one pearl bead.
17. Fold 15-inch wire in half. *You now have one set of 4 single beads, one set of 14 single beads and one set of 5 single beads. You also have one set of 10 crossovers, one set of 16 crossovers. Ending with a set of 4 beads and two wires.*
18. Center one pearl bead on wire.
19. Add one bead to each wire.
20. Crossover with one pearl bead.
21. Hold two wires together and add 33 pearl beads to both wires.
22. Add one pearl bead to each wire.
23. Crossover with one pearl bead.
24. Attach two pieces of the Treble Clef.
25. Using one wire from short piece and lower wire from long piece crossover in one pearl bead. Weave wires down through adjacent beads and crossover in one more pearl bead.
26. Weave each wire through closest bead to secure. Shape Treble Clef and attach at each intersection point.

Musical Notes

Upper Bar

1. Fold 15-inch wire in half. Center one pearl bead.
2. Add one pearl to each side.
3. Crossover with one pearl.
4. Repeat until you have 9 center beads.

Staff

1. Holding wires together add 20 pearls.

Note

1. Separate wires and crossover in one pearl bead.
2. Add on pearl to each side.
3. Crossover in one pearl
4. Add on pearl to each side.
5. Crossover in one pearl
6. Add on pearl to each side.
7. Crossover in one pearl
8. Back weave through previous two beads.
9. Add one pearl to each side.
10. Back weave through next outer beads.
11. Add on pearl to each side.
12. Back weave through next outer beads.
13. Secure wires.

Second Note

1. Add 11- inch wire by threading thru last 4 beads in upper bar.
2. Hold together and add 20 pearls.
3. Repeat instructions for note.

Bass Clef can be created by following the first portion of instructions for the treble clef then turning it upside down. The Bass clef should be half the size of the treble clef.

To suspend beads to the right, thread bead on wire leaving 1/4" space. Hold wires together and twist bead. Feed end of wire in and out of Bass Clef and repeat once. Back weave to secure.

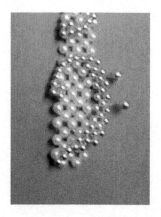

Ascension Lutheran Church 314 West Main Street
Danville, Virginia 24540 Phone: 434-792-5795
Web: chrismon.org Facebook, Pinterest, Etsy
E-mail: chrismonsministry@gmail.com
Copyright 2014 Lutheran Church of the Ascension, Danville, VA

Passion Cross

Difficulty: Beginner

Finished size: 4 inches

Beads:
  22 6mm gold
  54 4mm gold

Wire:
14 - inch 36 gauge gold
20 - inch 28 gauge gold

Chrismons

(CHRISt + MONogramS)

Latin Cross
With Trefoil

The Cross is always a reminder of our Lord's sacrifice for our sins, by which we receive forgiveness and salvation.

The white Trefoil represents the Holy Trinity, always with us.

Ascension Lutheran Church
Danville, Virginia

Small Passion Cross

22 6mm Gold beads
108 4mm Gold beads

14-inch 26 gauge gold wire
20-inch 28 gauge gold wire

Upright of Cross

1. String 3 4mm beads and loosely crossover 1 6mm bead in the center of the 28 gauge wire.
2. Gently turn center 4mm bead one full twist to create a pointed end to the cross.
3. Add 1 4mm bead to each wire and crossover with 1 6mm bead.
4. Repeat 12 times.
5. *There should be a total of 14 6mm beads on the upright of the cross.*
6. Add 1 4mm bead to each wire.
7. Thread both wires straight up into 1 more 4mm bead.
8. Take one wire under the 4mm bead and thread through the bead again and tighten.
9. Twist the two wires to create a hanger.

Arms of Cross

1. String 3 4mm beads and loosely crossover 1 6mm bead in the center of the 26 gauge wire.

2. Gently turn center 4mm bead one full twist to create a pointed end.
3. Add 1 4mm bead to each wire and crossover with 1 6mm bead.
4. Repeat 2 times.
5. *There should be a total of 4 6mm beads on each arm of the cross.*
6. Add 1 4mm bead to each wire.
7. Thread the two wires through the 5th and 6th large bead from the top of the upright.
8. Add 1 4mm bead to each wire and crossover with 1 6mm bead.
9. Repeat 3 times.
10. Add 3 4mm bead to one wire.
11. Gently twist center bead
12. Thread wire through opposite side of 6mm bead
13. Back weave until secure.

Chrismons™ Ornaments

✝ Ascension Lutheran Church 314 West Main Street
Danville, Virginia 24540 Phone: 434-792-5795
Web: chrismon.org Facebook, Pinterest, Etsy
E-mail: chrismonsministry@gmail.com
Copyright 2016 Lutheran Church of the Ascension, Danville, VA

Serpent on the Tau Cross

Difficulty: Intermediate

Finished size: 5.5 inches

Beads:

132 5x7mm pearls
2   4mm Bugle in gold
2   3mm gold
3   2mm gold
46 3x6mm gold
1   4x8mm gold

Wires:

4 12 - inch 28 gauge silver
4 16 - inch 28 gauge silver
   24-inch 28 gauge gold

Chrismons

(CHRISt + MONogramS)

Serpent on Tau Cross

Christ compared himself to an Old Testament story of Moses.

Just as Moses lifted up the snake in the desert, so the Son of Man must be lifted up, that everyone who believes in him may have eternal life. *John 3:14-15*

The LORD said to Moses, "Make a snake and put it up on a pole; any-one
who is bitten can look at it and live."
Numbers 21:8

The Tau Cross is an old testament Cross.

Ascension Lutheran Church
Danville, Virginia

Top Bar of Cross

1. Fold first 12-inch wire in half.
2. Place three 5x7mm beads on first wire.
3. Crossover with one 5x7mm bead
4. Repeat with second 12-inch wire.
5. Fold third 12-inch wire in half .
6. Place one 5x7mm beads on third wire.
7. Thread one side of third wire into one side bead of the first wire.
8. Thread other side of third wire into one side bead of the second wire.
9. Crossover with one 5x7mm bead.
10. Fold fourth 16-inch wire in half .
11. Place one 5x7mm bead on fourth wire.
12. Thread one side of fourth wire into the remaining side bead of the first wire and the other side of the fourth wire into the remaining side bead of the second wire.

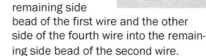

13. Crossover with one 5x7mm bead.
14. At this point you will have eight wires above 3 rows of 4 concentric beads.
15. Add four beads, one to each corner of double wires.
16. Crossover four beads using one wire from each corner.
17. Repeat until you have 7 boxes.
18. To end, return weave one wire from each corner.

Upright of Cross

1. Feed and center each 16" wire through one of the four bottom 5x7mm pearls of the center top square.
2. Add one 5x7mm bead to each set of corner wires.
3. Crossover in 5x7mm beads using one wire from each corner as before on top bar.

4. Repeat steps 3 and 4 until you have ten boxes below the cross bar.
5. To end, return weave all wires.

Serpent

1. Fold the 24 - inch 28 gauge wire in half. Center one 3mm gold on and hold bead twisting wire close bead.
2. String 46 3x6mm gold on both wires.
3. Crossover in one 3mm gold.
4. Add one 2mm gold to each wire .
5. Add one 4x8mm gold to both wires.
6. Add one 4mm bugle gold on each wire.
7. Return weave through the 4x8mm gold and use wires to begin securing serpent to cross.

Chrismons™ Ornaments

Ascension Lutheran Church 314 West Main Street
Danville, Virginia 24540 Phone: 434-792-5795
Web: chrismon.org Facebook, Pinterest, Etsy
E-mail: chrismonsministry@gmail.com
Copyright 2014 Lutheran Church of the Ascension, Danville, VA

Shepherd's Crook with Alpha & Omega

Difficulty: Beginner

Finished size: 5.5 inches

Beads:

  3 2mm gold

14 3mm gold

  1 4mm gold

   6 3mm pearl

 24 2mm pearl

Wire:

24 - inch 26 gauge gold

4 4 - inch 30 or 32 gauge
   gold

Chrismons

(CHRISt + MONogramS)

Shepherd's Crook with Alpha & Omega

The Alpha and Omega on the shepherd's crook show that this staff refers to the eternal one, the Good Shepherd.

The Chi Rho XP are also apparent in the design.

John 10:27-28

Ascension Lutheran Church
Danville, Virginia

Cross

1. Fold 24 inch 26 gauge wire in half and center 2mm bead.

2. Add one **3x6mm** gold on both wires.

3. String 10 **4x8mm** gold on both wires.

4. Add one **3mm** bead to both wires and separate wires.

5. Using left wire, add two **4x8mm** gold, one **3x6mm** gold and one **2mm** gold.

6. Return weave through the **3x6mm** and **4x8mm** gold to center.

7. Repeat steps 5 and 6 with right wire.

8. Cross over in one **3mm** gold.

9. Add one **3mm** gold to both wires.

10. String two **4x8mm** gold on both wires.

11. String four **3mm** gold both wires.

12. Separate wires and use right wire for following steps.

13. Feed 7 **3mm** gold and one **4mm** gold on right wire.

14. Return weave through **4mm** gold. Shape end to crook of

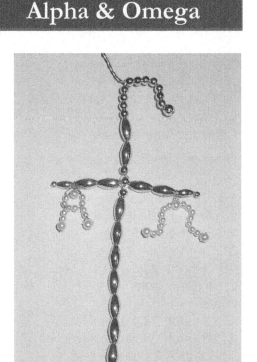

staff.

15. Twist wires to secure and create hanger.

Alpha and Omega

Using 4 pieces of 4 - inch 30 or 32 gauge gold wire and 2mm and 3mm pearl beads, follow directions for the Alpha and Omega on pages 42 and 43. Lowercase Omega shown in figure 3 from <u>The Chrismons Basic Series page 20</u> shown below.

Chrismons™ Ornaments

Ascension Lutheran Church 314 West Main Street
Danville, Virginia 24540 Phone: 434-792-5795
Web: chrismon.org, Facebook, Pinterest, Etsy
E-mail: chrismonsministry@gmail.com
Copyright 2016 Lutheran Church of the Ascension, Danville, VA

Tubular Cross

Difficulty: Intermediate

Finished size: 5.5 inches

Beads:

68   5mm pearl beads

64   5x7mm pearl beads

Wires:

4   18-inch 28 gauge silver

4   10-inch 28 gauge silver

Chrismons

(CHRISt + MONogramS)

Tubular Beaded Cross

The Cross is always a reminder of our Lord's sacrifice for our sins, by which we receive forgiveness and salvation.

Ascension Lutheran Church
Danville, Virginia

Upright of Cross

1. Center 1 5mm round bead on first 18-inch wire.
2. Center 1 round bead on second 18-inch wire.
3. Center 1 round bead on third 18-inch wire.
4. Center 1 round bead on fourth 18-inch wire.
5. Connect round bead 1 and round bead 2 by threading one wire from each bead into a 5x7 oval bead.
6. Add round bead 3 by threading second wire from
7. round bead 2 and one wire from round bead 3 into an oval bead.
8. Add round bead 4 by threading second wire from round bead 3
9. and one wire from round bead 4 into an oval bead.
10. Connect round bead 1 and round bead 4 by threading the
11. remaining wire from each into an oval bead.
12. Crossover one round bead above two oval beads using the two wires from bead one. Pull tight.
13. Crossover one round bead above two oval beads
14. using the two wires from bead two. Pull tight.
15. Crossover one round bead above two oval beads
16. using the two wires from bead three. Pull tight.
17. Crossover one round bead above two oval beads using the two wires from bead four. Pull tight.
18. Using the two wires at each corner add an oval bead.
19. Crossover 4 round beads using one wire from each adjacent oval bead.
20. Repeat until you have a column with 10 sets of oval beads. Ending with a set of round beads.
21. To end, return weave one wire from each corner. Use remaining four wires to create a hanger.

Arms of Cross

1. Center 1 5mm round bead on first 10-inch wire.
2. Center 1 round bead on second 10-inch wire.
3. Center 1 round bead on third 10-inch wire.

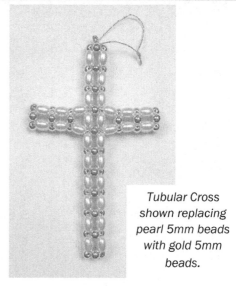

Tubular Cross shown replacing pearl 5mm beads with gold 5mm beads.

4. Center 1 round bead on fourth 10-inch wire.
5. Connect round bead 1 and round bead 2 by threading
6. one wire from each bead into a 5x7 oval bead.
7. Add round bead 3 by threading second wire from
8. round bead 2 and one wire from round bead 3 into an oval bead.
9. Add round bead 4 by threading second wire from round bead 3
10. and one wire from round bead 4 into an oval bead.
11. Connect round bead 1 and round bead 4 by threading the
12. remaining wire from each into an oval bead.
13. Crossover one round bead above two oval beads using the two wires from bead one.   Pull tight.
14. Crossover one round bead above two oval beads using the two wires from bead two.   Pull tight.
15. Crossover one round bead above two oval beads using the two wires from bead three. Pull tight.
16. Crossover one round bead above two oval beads using the two wires from bead four.   Pull tight.
17. Using the two wires at each corner add an oval bead.
18. Crossover 4 round beads using one wire from each adjacent oval bead.
19. Add 4 oval beads.
20. Thread 4 sets of corner wires into the front and back of the 4th and 5th round beads of the upright.
21. Add 3 sets of oval beads with crossovers. Ending with the round beads.
22. Return weave all eight wires to secure.

Chrismons™ Ornaments

Ascension Lutheran Church 314 West Main Street
Danville, Virginia 24540 Phone: 434-792-5795
Web: chrismon.org Facebook, Pinterest, Etsy
E-mail: chrismonsministry@gmail.com
Copyright 2014 Lutheran Church of the Ascension, Danville, VA

Tubular Bulbous Cross

Difficulty: Advanced

Finished size: 4 inches

Beads:

16 2mm pearl

20 3mm pearl

108 4mm pearl

16 5mm pearl

16 6mm Pearl

Wire:

4 20 - inch 36 gauge gold

4 12 - inch 28 gauge gold

Chrismons

(CHRISt + MONogramS)

Bulbar Tubular Cross

The Cross is always a reminder of our Lord's sacrifice for our sins, by which we receive forgiveness and salvation.

The Latin Cross is the most widely used form of the cross today.

The tubular design gives the design three dimensions.

Ascension Lutheran Church
Danville, Virginia

Upright of Cross
1. Center one 3mm bead on the first 20-inch wire.
2. Center one 3mm bead on the second 20-inch wire.
3. Crossover with one 2mm bead on each side of the 3mm bead.
4. Center one 2mm bead on the third 20-inch wire.
5. Add a 3mm bead to each side and crossover with one 4mm bead.
6. Repeat with the 4th wire.
7. Place third wire with 2mm bead between the 2mm beads from the first two wires.
8. Weave one wire from each 2mm bead into the 3mm bead on either side fo the third wire.
9. Crossover with one 4mm bead.
10. Weave one wire from each 2mm bead into the 3mm beads on either side of the third wire and crossover with one 4mm bead.

At this point you will have eight wires above 4 rows of beads.
Row 1 single 3mm bead.
Row 2 four 2mm beads
Row 3 four 3mm beads
Row 4 four 4mm beads

1. *Add four 6mm beads on each double wire in the corners.*
2. *Crossover with four 5mm beads.*
3. *Add four 4mm beads on each double wire in the corners.*
4. *Crossover with four 4mm beads.*
5. *Repeat until you have 17 sets of 4 - 4mm concentric beads. (9 corner beads)*
6. *Crossover with four 5mm beads.*
7. *Add four 6mm beads to the corners.*
8. *Crossover with four 4mm beads.*
9. *Add four 3mm beads.*
10. *Crossover with four 2mm beads.*
11. *Back weave with 4 wires.*
12. *Crossover remaining 4 wires in a single 3mm bead.*
13. *Twist wires to create a hanger.*

Crossbar
1. Center one 3mm bead on the first 12-inch wire.
2. Repeat with second 12-inch wire.
3. Crossover with one 2mm bead on each side of the 3mm bead.
4. Center one 2mm bead on the third 12-inch wire.
5. Add a 3mm bead to each side and cross-

over with one 4mm bead.
6. Repeat with fourth wire.
7. Place third wire with 2mm bead between the 2mm beads from the first two wires.
8. Weave one wire from each 2mm bead into the 3mm beads on either side of the third wire.
9. Crossover with one 4mm bead.
10. Weave one wire from each 2mm bead into the 3mm beads on either side of the third wire.
11. Crossover with one 4mm bead.

At this point you will have eight wires above 4 rows of beads as on the upright.

1. Add four 6mm beads on each double wire in the corners.
2. Crossover with four 5mm beads.
3. Add four 4mm beads on each double wire in the corners.
4. Weave 4 sets of wire into the 2nd and 3rd row of center 4mm beads from the top of the upright.
5. Add four 4mm beads on each double wire in the corners.
6. Crossover with four 4mm beads.
7. Add four 4mm beads on each double wire in the corners.
8. Crossover with four 5mm beads.
9. Add four 6mm to the corners.
10. Crossover with four 4mm beads.
11. Add four 3mm beads.
12. Crossover with four 2mm beads.
13. Back weave with 4 wires.
14. Crossover remaining 4 wires in a single 3mm bead.
15. Back weave to secure remaining wires.

Ascension Lutheran Church 314 West Main Street
Danville, Virginia 24540 Phone: 434-792-5795
Web: chrismon.org Facebook, Pinterest, Etsy
E-mail: chrismonsministry@gmail.com
Copyright 2016 Lutheran Church of the Ascension, Danville, VA

Difficulty: Advanced

Finished size: 4 inches

Beads:

    105 5mm pearl

    48 4mm pearl

    52 3mm pearl

Wire:

4 12 - inch 28 gauge gold

4 20 - inch 28 gauge gold

Chrismons

(CHRISt + MONogramS)

Tubular Passion Cross

The Cross is always a reminder of our Lord's sacrifice for our sins, by which we receive forgiveness and salvation.

The Latin Cross is the most widely used form of the cross today.

The pointed ends remind us of the wounds of Jesus.

The tubular design gives the design three dimensions.

Ascension Lutheran Church
Danville, Virginia

Upright of Cross

1. Fold first 20-inch wire in half.
2. Place three 3mm beads on first wire. Crossover with one 3mm bead.
3. Repeat with second 20-inch wire.
4. Fold third 20-inch wire in half.
5. Center one 3mm bead on the wire. Crossover with second 3mm bead.
6. Thread one side of third wire into one side bead of the first wire.
7. Thread other side of third wire into one side bead of the second wire. Crossover with one 3mm bead.
8. Fold fourth 20-inch wire in half.
9. Center one single bead at bottom of other 3 wires. Crossover in one 3mm bead.
10. Thread one side of fourth wire into the remaining side bead of the first wire and the other side of the fourth wire into the remaining side bead of the second wire.
11. Crossover with one 3mm bead. *At this point you*

will have eight wires above 3 rows of 4 concentric 3mm beads and a single 3mm bead at the point.

12. Add four 4mm beads, one to each corner of double wires. Cross over with four 4mm beads
13. Add four 4mm beads, one to each corner of double wires. Crossover with four 5mm beads using one wire from each corner.
14. Add four 5mm beads, one to each corner of double wires. Crossover with four 5mm beads using one wire from each corner.
15. Repeat until you have 19 concentric sets of 5mm

beads.

16. Add four **4mm** beads, one to each corner of double wires. Crossover with four **4mm** beads using one wire from each corner.
17. Add four **4mm** beads, one to each corner of double wires. Crossover with four **3mm** beads using one wire from each corner.
18. Add four **3mm** beads, one to each corner of double wires. Crossover with four **3mm** beads using one wire from each corner.
19. To end, return weave one wire fro m each corner. Use remaining four wires to crossover in one **3mm** bead and to create a hanger.

Arms of Cross

1. Fold first 12-inch wire in half.
2. Place three **3mm** beads on first wire. Crossover with one **3mm** Bead.
3. Repeat with second wire.
4. Fold third 12-inch wire in half.
5. Center one **3mm** bead on the wire. Crossover with second **3mm** bead.
6. Thread one side of third wire into one side bead of the first wire.
7. Thread other side of third wire into one side bead of the second wire. Cross over with one **3mm** bead.
8. Fold fourth 12-inch wire in half.
9. Center one single bead at bottom of other 3 wires. Crossover in one **3mm** bead.
10. Thread one side of fourth wire into the remaining side bead of the first wire and the other side of the fourth wire into the remaining side bead of the second wire. Crossover with one **3mm** bead. *At this point you will have eight*

wires above 3 rows of 4 concentric 3mm beads and a single bead 3mm bead at the point.

11. Add four **4mm** beads, one to each corner of double wires. Crossover with four **4mm** beads using one wire from each corner.
12. Add four **4mm** beads, one to each corner of double wires. Crossover with four **5mm** beads using one wire from each corner.
13. Add four **5mm** beads, one to each corner of double wires. Crossover with four **5mm** beads using one wire from each corner.
14. Add four **5mm** beads, one to each corner of double wires. Weave wires through upright at the 3rd and 4th **5mm** beads from the top.
15. Add four **5mm** beads, one to each corner of double wires. Crossover with four **5mm** beads using one wire from each corner.
16. Repeat one time.
17. Add four **4mm** beads, one to each corner of double wires. Crossover with four **4mm** beads using one wire from each corner.
18. Add four **4mm** beads, one to each corner of double wires. Crossover with four **3mm** beads using one wire from each corner.
19. Add four **3mm** beads, one to each corner of double wires. Crossover with four **3mm** beads using one wire from each corner.
20. To end, return weave one wire from each corner. Use remaining four wires to crossover in one **3mm** bead and return weave to secure.

Chrismons™ Ornaments

Ascension Lutheran Church 314 West Main Street
Danville, Virginia 24540 Phone: 434-792-5795
Web: chrismon.org Facebook, Pinterest, Etsy
E-mail: chrismonsministry@gmail.com
Copyright 2016 Lutheran Church of the Ascension, Danville, VA

Wedding Ring Cross

Difficulty: Advanced

Finished size: 4 inches

Beads:

58 3mm gold

8 2mm gold

64 3x6 pearl

72 3mm pearl

Wire:

4 16 - inch 28 gauge silver

4 12 - inch 28 gauge silver

1 18 - inch 28 gauge gold

Chrismons

(CHRISt + MONogramS)

Wedding Cross

The Cross is always a reminder of Our Lord's sacrifice

Two wedding rings embedded in the upright of a Cross represent the couple whose marriage has a firm foundation in Christ.

The arms of the Cross over the rings represent Jesus' blessing of the union.

Ascension Lutheran Church

Danville, Virginia

Interlocking Wedding Rings. GOLD

1. Add 1 **3mm**, 1 **2mm**, 20 **3mm**, 1 **2mm**, 1 **3mm**, 1 **2mm**, 8 **3mm**, 1 **2mm** to 18-inch wire.
2. Reweave the wire through everything a second time **do not** pull the two loops tight.
3. Weave through the 1st **3mm** bead for a third time.
4. Add 1 **2mm**, 8 **3mm**, 1 **2mm** to 1 wire.
5. CC in **3mm** between 2 **2mm** beads.

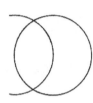

6. Pull both wires slightly.
7. Using one wire add 1 **2mm**, 10 **3mm**, using second do same thing in opposite direction. Weave each wire through beads on other wire.
8. CC each wire in **3mm** at top and bottom of Vesica Piscis.
9. Weave both wires into 1 **2mm** and 4 or 5 of the 8 **3mm** beads to secure.

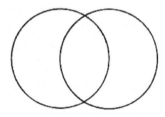

Tubular Cross PEARL

Upright of Cross

1. Fold first 16-inch wire in half.
2. Center 1 **3mm** bead, add 1 **3x6**

to each side.

3. Crossover with one **3mm** bead.
4. Repeat with second wire.
5. Fold third 16-inch wire in half .
6. Place one **3mm** bead on third wire.
7. Thread one side of third wire into one **3x6** bead of the first wire.
8. Thread other side of third wire into one **3x6** bead of the second wire.
9. Crossover with one **3mm** bead.
10. Fold fourth 16-inch wire in half .
11. Place one **3mm** bead on fourth wire.
12. Thread one side of fourth wire into the remaining **3x6** bead of the first wire and the other side of the fourth wire into the remaining **3x6** bead of the second wire.
13. Crossover with one **3mm** bead.
14. *At this point you will have eight wires above 1 circle of 3mm beads, one circle of 3x6 beads*

and one circle of **3mm** beads.

15. Add four **3x6** beads, one to each corner of double wires.

16. Crossover four 3mm beads using one wire from each corner.

Add Wedding Rings

1. Add four **3x6** beads, one to each corner of double wires.

2. Crossover 1 **3mm** bead on front of cross and 1 **3mm** bead on back of cross.

3. Center wedding rings between front and back of cross.

4. Fold Rings Down.

5. Crossover with **3mm** bead through the left ring.

6. Crossover with **3mm** bead through the right ring.

7. Add four **3x6** beads, one to each corner of double wires. Crossover four **3mm** beads using one wire from each corner.

8. Repeat

9. Add four **3x6** beads, one to each corner of double wires. Crossover 1 **3mm** bead on front of cross and 1 **3mm** bead on back of cross.

10. Bring rings back up and center wedding rings between front and back of cross.

11. Crossover with **3mm** bead over the left ring.

12. Crossover with **3mm** bead over the right ring.

13. Add four **3x6** beads, one to each corner of double wires.

14. Crossover four **3mm** beads using one wire from each corner. *At this point you have 7 sets of 3x6 beads.*

Create center of Cross

1. Add four **3mm** beads, one to each corner of double wires. Crossover four **3mm** beads using one wire from each corner.

2. Add four **3x6** beads, one to each corner of double wires. Crossover four **3mm** beads using one wire from each corner.

3. Repeat 2 times. *At this point you have 7 sets of 3x6 beads, 1 set of 3mm beads and 3 sets of 3x6 beads.*

4. To end, return weave one wire from each corner. Use remaining four wires to create a hanger.

Arms of Cross

1. Fold first 12-inch wire in half. Center 1 **3mm** bead, add 1 **3x6** to each side. Crossover with one **3mm** bead.

2. Fold second 12-inch wire in half. Center 1 **3mm** bead, add 1 **3x6** to each side. Crossover with one **3mm** bead.

3. Fold third 12-inch wire in half. Place one **3mm** bead on third wire.

4. Thread one side of third wire into one **3x6** bead of the first wire.

5. Thread other side of third wire into one **3x6** bead of the second wire.

6. Crossover with one **3mm** bead.

7. Fold fourth 12-inch wire in half. Place one **3mm** bead on fourth wire.

8. Thread one side of fourth wire into the remaining **3x6** bead of the first wire and the other side of the fourth wire into the remaining **3x6** bead of the second wire.

9. Crossover with one **3mm** bead. *At this point you will have eight wires above 1 circle of 3mm beads, one circle of 3x6 beads and one circle of 3mm beads.*

10. Add four **3x6** beads, one to each corner of double wires. Crossover four **3mm** beads using one wire from each corner.

11. Add four **3x6** beads, one to each corner of double wires.

12. Weave corners through center set of **3mm** on upright.

13. Add four **3x6** beads, one to each corner of double wires. Crossover four 3mm beads using one wire from each corner.

14. Repeat twice.

15. To end, return weave one wire from each corner. Return weave all eight wires to secure.

Chrismons
(CHRISt + MONogramS)

Alpha Lambda Cross With four Crosslets

In the beginning was the Word,
and the Word was with God and the Word
was God. *John 1:1*

Alpha is the first letter of the Greek alphabet
and reminds us of the beginning. Lambda is
the first letter of the Greek *Logos* - Word.

The four crosslets represent the Great Commission. The crossbar of the A reminds us of
outstretched arms.

Go therefore and make disciples of all the
nations, baptizing them in the name of the
Father and the Son and the Holy Spirit,
teaching them to observe all that I have commanded you. And behold, I am with you
always, to the end of the age. *Matthew 28:19-20*

Ascension Lutheran Church
Danville, Virginia

Chrismons
(CHRISt + MONogramS)

A Mother's Love
Cross, Heart and Love

The original of this design was created by
Mrs. Francis Spencer from the beads of a
carved ivory necklace that her mother
wore when Mrs. Spencer was a child.

Mary treasured up all these things and
pondered them in her heart. *Luke 2:19*

Love the Lord your God with all your
heart and with all your soul and with all
your strength and with all your mind; and
Love your neighbor as yourself. *Luke 10:27*

Ascension Lutheran Church
Danville, VA

Chrismons
(CHRISt + MONogramS)

The Anchor Cross or Cross of Hope

This Child,
the hope of the world.
A cross rises out of the crescent moon,
a symbol for Mary, our Lord's mother.

Ascension Lutheran Church
Danville, VA

Chrismons
(CHRISt + MONogramS)

Budded Greek Cross or Greek Cross Voided

The Greek cross has four equal arms representing the four corners of the earth,
the four directions on the compass, or
the four winds. Jesus brought salvation
to people from ever direction and nation.
Mark 13:26 - 27

The triple bud on the end of each arm of
the cross reminds us of the Trinity. We
are made children of the Triune God;
Father, Son, and Holy Spirit, through our
Baptism. *Matthew 28:19 - 20*

Ascension Lutheran Church
Danville, VA

Cards are 3 x 5 in. to frame on a background just under 4 x 6 inches to fit in a clear bag. Permission to copy for personal use.

Chrismons
(CHRISt + MONogramS)

CELTIC CROSS

Latin Cross with Everlasting circle and Vine.

The Latin Cross: A reminder of our Lord's sacrifice.

The Circle: Always a symbol of our Lord's everlasting love. The original meaning may have been the sun, a welcome sign in a northern climate or a symbol of unity. It may also simple have been to hold up the heavy arms of the cross.

The Ornamentation: Elaborate carvings adorn many ancient Celtic Crosses. Basket weaves, medallions, serpents and vines. The vine here represents the true vine, rooted in the Trinity.

Ascension Lutheran Church
Danville, Virginia

Chrismons
(CHRISt + MONogramS)

XP
Chi Rho

The first letters of Christ (CHR) in the Greek Alphabe. XPIOTOS or Christos

Or

The initials for Christ the King in Latin Christus Rex

Most of the monograms of Christ Jesus are based on Greek words. The first two letters, Chi and Rho are superimposed on each other, to create this Chrismons.

Ascension Lutheran Church
Danville, VA

Chrismons
(CHRISt + MONogramS)

XP
Chi Rho in Eternity

The first letters of Christ (CHR) in the Greek Alphabe. XPIOTOS or Christos

Or

The initials for Christ the King in Latin Christus Rex

Christ wrapped in a never ending circle, representing God's everlasting love.

Ascension Lutheran Church
Danville, VA

Chrismons
(CHRISt + MONogramS)

50th Anniversary Cross
1957 - 2006

The Latin cross a reminder of our Lord's sacrifice for our sins, by which we receive forgiveness and salvation.

The Rose a reminder of our Lord's virgin mother Mary, His human birth, or His humanity.

The Butterfly a reminder of our Lord's resurrection and the resurrection of those who die in Christ.

1 Corinthians 15:20—23

Ascension Lutheran Church
Danville, VA

Chrismons
(CHRISt + MONogramS)

Chrismons 50th Anniversary Gift Cross 1957 - 2006

The Latin Cross: A reminder of our Lord's sacrifice.

This cross was given to the congregation of Ascension Lutheran Church in remembrance of the fiftieth anniversary of the Chrismons Ministry.

Ascension Lutheran Church
Danville, Virginia

Chrismons
(CHRISt + MONogramS)

Christ the King Cross & Crown

The Latin cross a reminder of our Lord's sacrifice for our sins, by which we receive forgiveness and salvation.

The Crown reminds of us the Kingship of our Lord, Jesus Christ, The **King** of Kings and **Lord** of lords.

1 Timothy 6:15

Ascension Lutheran Church
Danville, VA

Chrismons
(CHRISt + MONogramS)

Christ's Monograms

The initials and abbreviations of Christ are incorporated within the center design of the cross.

The first letters of Christ (CHR) in the Greek Alphabet XPIOTOS or Christos Chi Rho (XP or XPC)

IC or IS and The initials for Christ the King in Latin Christus Rex

Ascension Lutheran Church
Danville, VA

Chrismons
(CHRISt + MONogramS)

Cross in Gloria

The rising sun behind the Cross suggests a new day when our Lord conquered death for us.

Cross
with Nimbus and Rays

Latin Cross: A reminder of our Lord's sacrifice.

Nimbus: A circle of light around the head that connotes Godliness or holiness.

Rays: Light - "I am the light of the world" John 8:12

Ascension Lutheran Church
Danville, VA

Cards are 3 x 5 in. to frame on a background just under 4 x 6 inches to fit in a clear bag.   Permission to copy for personal use.

Chrismons
(CHRISt + MONogramS)

Cross of Constantine

The Chi Rho is part of the legend of how Constantine became the first Roman emperor to embrace Christianity. During a definitive battle for the city of Rome Constantine saw a sign in the sky with the words,

"In this sign conquer."

Whether the sign he saw was the cross or the Greek abbreviation for Christ is unknown. But it is certain that, after that military campaign was successfully concluded, he placed the Chi Rho symbol on his labarum or imperial standard. Thus the Chi Rho became associated with triumph. In addition to the original Greek meaning, a Latin interpretation was given to the letters –*Christus Rex* or Christ, the King

Ascension Lutheran Church
Danville, VA

Chrismons
(CHRISt + MONogramS)

Cross Triumphant

A cross supreme over the world symbolizes the triumph of the Savior over the sin of the world.

The world united in Christ who has dominion over all.

Ascension Lutheran Church
Danville, VA

Example of gift card with ornament

Chrismons
(CHRISt + MONogramS)

The Anchor Cross or
Cross of Hope

This Child,
the hope

A cross rises out of the
a symbol for Mary, our L

nsion Lutheran
Danville,

Cards are 3 x 5 in. to frame on a background just under 4 x 6 inches to fit in a clear bag. Permission to copy for personal use.

Chrismons

(CHRISt + MONogramS)

9 Point Crown

The Crown is a symbol for the Kingship of our Lord, Jesus Christ,

the King of kings and Lord of lords.

1 Timothy 6:15

Ascension Lutheran Church
Danville, VA

Chrismons

(CHRISt + MONogramS)

Page 54 Crown

The Kingship of our Lord; His Victory over sin and death; His Place of honor at the right hand of the Father.

Named for the photo in the Chrismons explanation booklet, page 54

Ascension Lutheran Church
Danville, VA

Chrismons

(CHRISt + MONogramS)

Iota Chi

IX

The Iota (I) is the first letter of our Lord's given name Jesus in Greek. This name means "the promised one."

The Chi(X) is the first letter of his Greek title Christ. Christos (XPISTOS), is the translation of the Hebrew "Messiah", which means "the one anointed by God."

When these two letters are superimposed, they become our Savior's cipher, the symbolic interweaving of initials that some people call a star.

Ascension Lutheran Church
Danville, Virginia

Chrismons

(CHRISt + MONogramS)

Iota Chi in Eternity

Jesus Christ at the center of God's everlasting love.

IX and Circle

The Iota (I) is the first letter of our Lord's given name Jesus in Greek. This name means "the promised one."

The Chi (X) is the first letter of his Greek title Christos, "the one anointed by God."

The never ending circle represents God's everlasting love for us.

Ascension Lutheran Church
Danville, Virginia

Cards are 3 x 5 in. to frame on a background just under 4 x 6 inches to fit in a clear bag. Permission to copy for personal use.

Chrismons
(CHRISt + MONogramS)
Greek Cross
With
Iota Eta Sigma

The first three letters of JESUS in Greek compose this monogram.

i h c

The monogram hangs on a Greek Cross to remind us of our Savior's sacrifice for all mankind.

Ascension Lutheran Church
Danville, Virginia

Chrismons
(CHRISt + MONogramS)

Jesus Cross

The Cross is always a reminder of our Lord's saving work of redeeming mankind through His sacrifice for our sins, by which we receive forgiveness and salvation.

The Latin Cross is the most widely used form of the cross today.

The Cross of Jesus is filled with God's Eternal Love.

The Last Supper

Ascension Lutheran Church
Danville, VA

Chrismons
(CHRISt + MONogramS)

Latin Cross

The Cross is always a reminder of our Lord's saving work of redeeming mankind through His sacrifice for our sins, by which we receive forgiveness and salvation.

The Latin Cross is the most widely used form of the cross today.

Ascension Lutheran Church
Danville, VA

Chrismons
(CHRISt + MONogramS)

Latin Cross
With Hanging
Alpha & Omega

The Cross is always a reminder of our Lord's saving work of redeeming mankind through His sacrifice for our sins, by which we receive forgiveness and salvation

The Hanging Alpha and Omega remind us

"I am Alpha and the Omega, the first and the last, the beginning and the end". Revelations 22:13; Isaiah 44:6; Isaiah 48:12.

Ascension Lutheran Church
Danville, Virginia

Cards are 3 x 5 in. to frame on a background just under 4 x 6 inches to fit in a clear bag. Permission to copy for personal use.

Chrismons
(CHRISt + MONogramS)

Flared Latin Cross

The Cross is always a reminder of our Lord's saving work of redeeming mankind through His sacrifice for our sins, by which we receive forgiveness and salvation.

The Latin Cross is the most widely used form of the cross today.

Ascension Lutheran Church
Danville, Virginia

Chrismons
(CHRISt + MONogramS)

Latin Cross
With Trefoil

The Cross is always a reminder of our Lord's sacrifice for our sins, by which we receive forgiveness and salvation.

The white Trefoil represents the Holy Trinity, always with us.

Ascension Lutheran Church
Danville, Virginia

Chrismons
(CHRISt + MONogramS)

Passion Cross
with
Alpha and Omega

The paired Latin Crosses Fusilee, one entwined with an Alpha another with an Omega remind us

"I am Alpha and the Omega,
the first and the last,
the beginning and the end".
Revelations 22:13; Isaiah 44:6; Isaiah 48:12.

The pointed ends of the Cross Fusilee, also known as the Passion Cross
(or Cross of Suffering), remind us of the points of the thorns, the nails, and the spear.
John 19.

Ascension Lutheran Church
Danville, Virginia

Chrismons
(CHRISt + MONogramS)

The Maltese Cross
St. John's Cross

Four Arms of the Cross
Four Cardinal Virtues
Prudence Temperance
Justice   Fortitude

The eight points stand for
The Beatitudes *Matthew 5:1-11*
or
The Obligations of a Knight
Live in truth. Have faith.
Be sincere. Give proof of humility.
Love justice. Be merciful.
Endure persecution.
Repent of sin.

Ascension Lutheran Church
Danville, Virginia

Cards are 3 x 5 in. to frame on a background just under 4 x 6 inches to fit in a clear bag.   Permission to copy for personal use.

Chrismons
(CHRISt + MONogramS)

Music Cross

Sing
&
Make Music
In Your
Heart to the Lord

Speak to one another with psalms, hymns and spiritual songs. Always giving thanks to God the Father for everything, in the name of our Lord Jesus Christ.

Ephesians 5:19-20

Ascension Lutheran Church
Danville, VA

Chrismons
(CHRISt + MONogramS)

Passion Cross

The Cross is always a reminder of our Lord's sacrifice for our sins, by which we receive forgiveness and salvation.

The Latin Cross is the most widely used form of the cross today.

The pointed ends remind us of the wounds of Jesus.

Ascension Lutheran Church
Danville, Virginia

Chrismons
(CHRISt + MONogramS)

Serpent on Tau Cross

Christ compared himself to an Old Testament story of Moses.

Just as Moses lifted up the snake in the desert, so the Son of Man must be lifted up, that everyone
who believes in him may have eternal life.
John 3:14-15

The LORD said to Moses, "Make a snake and put it up on a pole; anyone who is bitten can look at it and live."
Numbers 21:8

The Tau Cross is an old testament Cross.

Ascension Lutheran Church
Danville, Virginia

Chrismons
(CHRISt + MONogramS)

Shepherd's Crook with Alpha & Omega

The Alpha and Omega on the shepherd's crook show that this staff refers to the eternal one, the Good Shepherd.

The Chi Rho XP are also apparent in the design.

John 10:27-28

Ascension Lutheran Church
Danville, Virginia

Cards are 3 x 5 in. to frame on a background just under 4 x 6 inches to fit in a clear bag. Permission to copy for personal use.

Chrismons
(CHRISt + MONogramS)

Tubular Beaded Cross

The Cross is always a reminder of our Lord's sacrifice for our sins, by which we receive forgiveness and salvation.

Ascension Lutheran Church
Danville, Virginia

Chrismons
(CHRISt + MONogramS)

Bulbar Tubular Cross

The Cross is always a reminder of our Lord's sacrifice for our sins, by which we receive forgiveness and salvation.

The Latin Cross is the most widely used form of the cross today.

The tubular design gives the design three dimensions.

Ascension Lutheran Church
Danville, Virginia
Danville, VA

Chrismons
(CHRISt + MONogramS)

Tubular Passion Cross

The Cross is always a reminder of our Lord's sacrifice for our sins, by which we receive forgiveness and salvation.

The Latin Cross is the most widely used form of the cross today.

The pointed ends remind us of the wounds of Jesus.

The tubular design gives the design three dimensions.

Ascension Lutheran Church
Danville, Virginia

Chrismons
(CHRISt + MONogramS)

Wedding Cross

The Cross is always a reminder of Our Lord's sacrifice

Two wedding rings embedded in the upright of a Cross represent the couple whose marriage has a firm foundation in Christ.

The arms of the Cross over the rings represent Jesus' blessing of the union.

Ascension Lutheran Church
Danville, Virginia

Cards are 3 x 5 in. to frame on a background just under 4 x 6 inches to fit in a clear bag. Permission to copy for personal use.

Chrismons   Books

The Basic Series

Patterns for monograms and symbols for our Lord and God.   Some information in this book is not repeated in the other books, making it essential to understanding everything in the other series.   34 Designs, 73 Pages ISBN#978-0-0975472-0-9 **$14.95**

Chrismons for Every Day

Introduces miniatures, beginner projects and a set of eight designs of The Beatitudes. Includes patterns, directions, and ideas, for using Chrismons throughout the year as bookmarks, wedding-cake toppers, pictures, arrangements, mobiles and wreaths. For beginner and advanced workers. *69 pages ISBN#978-0-9715472-3-0* **$14.95**

The Christian Year Series

Based on the Liturgical Church Year. (Advent, Christmas, Epiphany, Lent, Easter, Ascension, Pentecost,) there are 30 designs in this Group. We here at Ascension use the Christian Year's series as a focal point of our tree. *65 Pages ISBN#978-0-0975472-1-6* **$14.95**

The Advanced Series

Sixty new designs of Chrismons including the popular Parable Balls series, Angels & Archangels, Individual symbols, and Trees. Easy to make, there are is no duplication of the designs in any of the series. *69 Pages ISBN#978-0-9715472-2-3* **$14.95**

Chrismons

This book contains a condensed interpretation for most of the ornaments on our Church's Chrismons Tree. 54 Pages ISBN# 978-0-9715472-4-7 **$9.95**

Samuel Sparrow and The Tree of Light Children's Storybook
28 Pages Library of Congress #2003107199 ISBN#978-0-9715472-5-4 **$6.00**

Page 54 Crown

These directions are for the crown on page 54 of the Explanation book (Chrismons). PLEASE NOTE: The Small church and home sizes of these patterns are now available in the Chrismons for Everyday Series and the Crosses and Crowns Home Size Chrismons Book. *$2.00*

***Contact us for* current prices and shipping rates**

Crosses And Crowns

A home sized version of our most popular cross and crown Chrismons designs. Easy to follow format with complete material lists and step by step explanations. *75 pages   ISBN#978-0-9715472-7-8* **$14.95**

Chrismons Cross Stitch Patterns

Original Chrismons designs adapted for cross stitch by The Peer Collection with permission from Ascension Lutheran Church, Danville, VA. for nonprofit use only.

Cross Stitch Chrismons:

12 of our designs in cross stitch patterns **$5.00**

DVD
Explanation of the Chrismons Tree **$10.00**

A visual visit to the Chrismons tree with an up close look at some of our most significant Chrismons Ornaments.

CD
Instructions for 5 easy to make cross Chrismons in power point **$10.00**
Note: All five crosses are also included in the Crosses and Crowns book.

Item	Qty	Price
The Basic Series 34 Designs, 73 pgs. *ISBN#978-0-0975472-0-9*	_____ X	$14.95
Chrismons for Every Day 69 pages *ISBN#978-0-9715472-3-0*	_____ X	$14.95
The Christian Year Series 65 Pages *ISBN#978-0-0975472-1-6*	_____ X	$14.95
The Advanced Series 69 Pages *ISBN#978-0-9715472-2-3*	_____ X	$14.95
Chrismons Explanations Book 54 pgs. *ISBN# 978-0-9715472-4-7*	_____ X	$9.95
Page 54 Crown Instructions Directions to make the Crown shown on page 54 of the ***Chrismons*** *Explanation Book.*	_____ X	$2.00
Samuel Sparrow and The Tree of Light Children's Story Book 28 Pages Library of Congress #2003107199 ISBN#978-0-9715472-5-4	_____ X	$6.00
Complete Set—all books above	_____ X	$70.00
Crosses & Crowns 72 Pages *ISBN#978-0-9715472-7-8*	_____ X	$14.95
Cross Stitch Chrismons *Directions for 12 designs*	_____ X	$5.00
DVD Explanation of Chrismons Tree	_____ X	$10.00
CD Directions for 5 Chrismons Crosses in PowerPoint format.	_____ X	$10.00
Domestic Shipping Charges Priority Mail Flat Rate 1-6 items $5.75, 7-12 items $12.35		$_____
Total Enclosed		$_____

In the tradition of Chrismons, we do not sell finished ornaments, however we do make the patterns available to assist you in making the ornaments and sharing this ministry with others. This is a non-profit ministry. Contact the church for the current prices, or to purchase directly from the church.

Our books are also available online through our Etsy store www.etsy.com/shop/chrismons

chrismon.org · chrismonsministry@gmail.com

The History of Chrismons™

CHRISMONS™ ornaments were originate and first made for use on the Christmas tree of Ascension Lutheran Church in Danville, Virginia, in 1957 by Mrs. Frances Kipps Spencer, a church member. The designs are monograms of and symbols for our Lord Jesus Christ. Because these designs have been used by his followers since biblical times, they are the heritage of all Christians and serve to remind each of us regardless of denomination of the One we follow. All Chrismons™ ornaments are made in a combination of white and gold to symbolize the purity and majesty of the Son of God and the Son of Man.

The Chrismons™ Tree tradition has continued at Ascension Lutheran Church for over fifty years. Mrs. Spencer stated a tree was never finished until someone came to see it and have the story of Christ explained to them through the ornaments. Today the original ornaments are joined by gifts from around the globe.

Viewing the Tree:

The tree is available for viewing from approximately the second week in December through Christmas Eve. Live interpreters are on site to explain the tree every evening between 7 pm and 9 pm. Sundays we offer an afternoon visit from 3 pm to 5 pm and the 7 pm - 9 pm session. Groups are welcome to schedule a day-time visit by contacting the Chrismons™ Secretary at 434-792-5795.

All of the Chrismons™ books are copyrighted by the Lutheran Church of the Ascension, 314 West Main Street, Danville, Virginia. As holders of the properties of the church, our trustees have authorized me to grant a limited, non-exclusive license of copyrights. At no time will our church permit any institution, person or corporation to make for profit from the sale of Chrismons™ books. We charge a fee for the instruction books which covers postage, handling and printing only. It is the policy of our church that the Chrismons™ books shall not become a fun raising or profit making activity.

With these limitations in mind, we hereby give you permission to use copyrighted materials as the basis for the preparation and distribution of explanations about Chrismons™ symbols, provided you in no way change or distort the original meaning. This limited license is valid only as long as instructions or information describing Chrismons™ symbols are not sold, used to raise money, or used in any manner for the profit-making venture.

Chrismons™ is the trademark of the Lutheran Church of the Ascension for its printed publications and may not be used as a trademark for printed matter by any other party.

May God bless you in spreading the gospel of His Love and His redemptive Act through His Son-not only through the use of Chrismons™ symbols but in every aspect of your work and life.

Sincerely,

Kate Albright, Karen Distad

Directors of the Chrismons™ Ministry

Ascension Lutheran Church Chrismons™ Ministry

Our tree is open to the public for viewing from approximately the second week in December through Christmas Eve each year.

314 West Main Street ♦ Danville, Virginia 24541

We're on the web @ www.chrismon.org
facebook.com/ChrismonsMinistry
pinterest.com/chrismons/
etsy.com/shop/chrismons

The Making of a Chrismons Tree

Evergreen cedar trees grow in this part of Virginia so that is our tree of choice.

A search committee starts looking in the summer.

The tree must have a single trunk tree with a full shape that does not need filler.

The tree must be accessible with a trailer.

Every Chrismons Tree has been donated by the owners.

On a Friday in late November or early December volunteers go out to the site and harvest the tree. The side that will be the front of the tree is marked with a tag before the tree is cut down.

The tree is carried back to the church and rolled onto the lawn where it stays overnight.